I Once Knew Vincent

Michelle Rene

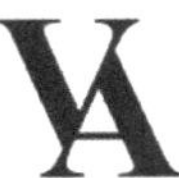

Vabella Publishing
P.O. Box 1052
Carrollton, Georgia 30112

13-digit ISBN 978-1-983230-62-2

Library of Congress Control Number 2014900078

10 9 8 7 6 5 4 3 2 1

Dedicated with love to my mother, Donna, my husband, Brian,
and my son, Aiden.

A special thanks goes to all my supportive friends and family,
especially Shell and Cathy. You were my first fans.

A Note from the Author

The people in this book were real people, and the events in this book are based on actual events. However, while this story was inspired by actual events, it is a work of fiction. Some facts have been changed and some events have been added for the sake of storytelling.

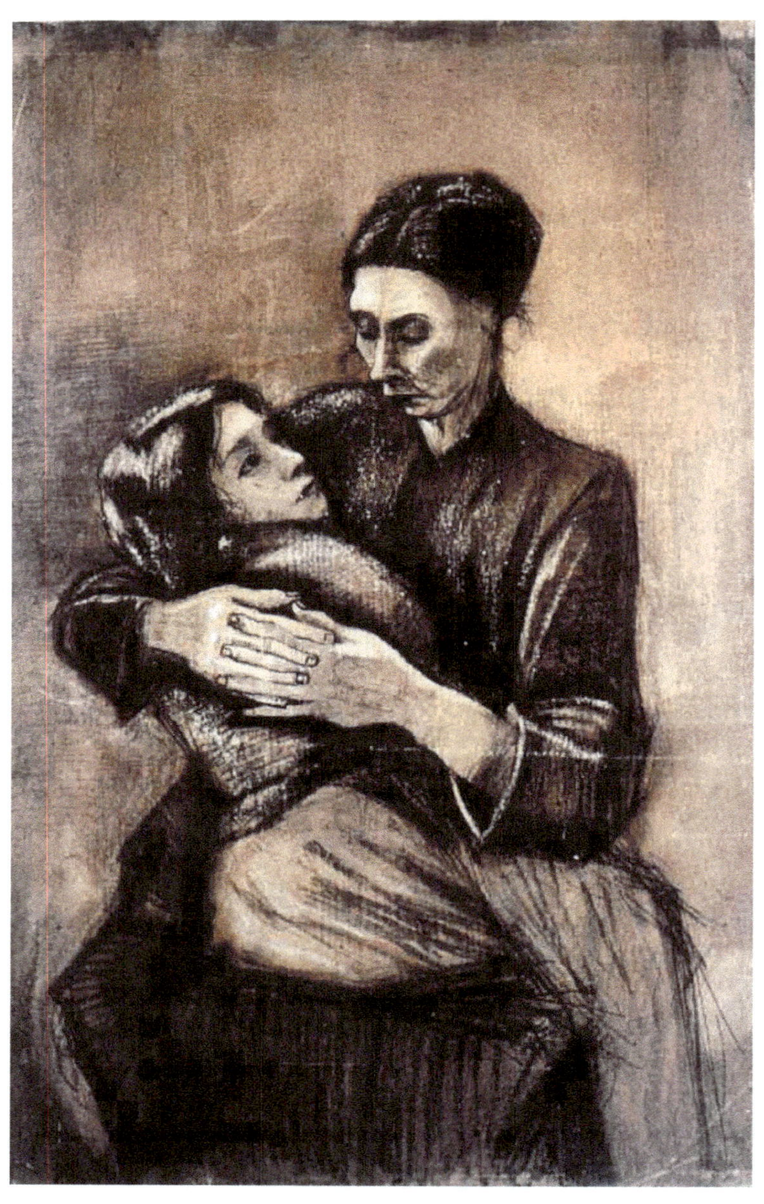

*"I put my heart and my soul into my work
and have lost my mind in the process."*

\- Vincent Van Gogh

Chapter One

I am an honest woman, and because of that fact, I was an equally honest girl. As a grown woman looking back on my childhood, I can see that honesty was not always considered a valuable trait or even a virtuous trait in young women. The manner of my honesty often exasperated matters. I coated very little with the sweet tongue of honey as was the custom for young ladies of my time. To be very plain, I had very little use for such practices.

In the late nineteenth century, The Hague was a center for Dutch artists and dealers who helped deliver unto the world a new era in revolutionary painting. This was true for the countless struggling artists and art dealers that lived and worked there. It was a center for an explosion of expression that was shadowed only by the even larger revolution happening in Paris.

However, my moeder and I knew nothing of the major artistic strides created in our fair city because my moeder was an alcoholic whore. I did say that I was honest, so it should be understood that I would not label her as such to purely insult her. The plain truth was that she sold her body to feed us in times of great need. To cope with her intense misery and sorrow, she would turn to the comforts of liquor.

My moeder was named Clasina Maria Hoornik, but no one actually called her Clasina. Anyone who really knew her referred to her as Sien. To me, she was Moeder. She had been Moeder to two other children, but they had not lived. The first was a girl made so frail and tired by Sien's lack of nutrition that the turmoil of birth was too much for her to bear. The baby was born early, and she was born already dead. The second was a boy that my Moeder named Wilhelmus Hoornik. He too was weak and frail, and when Sien's body became unable to produce milk for him any longer, he too died after only one year of life.

Losing babies was not uncommon for women as poor as my moeder, and I was so young that I did not remember the loss of the first child. The second child however, little Wilhelmus, I do remember. I was only a very young child myself, but I do have some blurry colored memories of holding his little body in my arms. I remember feeling how light he seemed, lighter than a baby ought to be.

I could not help but wonder why it was that I was the one strong enough to survive when others wasted away. Was I cursed or privileged to be strong enough to survive this world? Sometimes, in moments of great terror, I thought that it would have been easier to fade away as they had. When faced with the intense need of hunger, such things are easy to think.

The Hague was the city, and with the city came the smells of the city. If we walked down almost any street, we would encounter the sights and smells of everything real that we could not afford. From the scent of the newly dyed cloth to the warm fragrance of the food merchants, everything we saw was only available if we had the coins. Of course, we had none. The fine linens hanging in the window were only for show, and the fresh milk and cheese at the dairy man's booth could only be wanted from afar.

The worst for me was when we passed the smoke house. I loved meat so very much. The smell of smoked pork and beef aroused a yearning in me that could be surpassed by nothing else as far as I was concerned. It was a deep want that was rarely satisfied.

Meat was a luxury. On the rare occasion that I did receive a bit of meat, it was a gift; a rare and beautiful present that I savored for as long as I could manage. For the most part, we ate bread when we were able to eat at all. Sometimes, Moeder managed to get some milk with our bread. Once in a great while, there was cheese and even a potato, but black bread soaked in water to soften it was normally our supper.

Normally, Sien worked as a seamstress, and she even tried to work as a charwoman like her mother, the woman whose name I bore. However, her ugly appearance, sorrowful demeanor, and reputation for prostitution limited her employment opportunities in The Hague.

She lost most of the reputable charwoman positions to young, pious girls with clean, round faces. All were devout Catholics or Protestants from good families. Sien prayed but never took to religion the way the devout did, and her apathy to it made people wary of her. Be a girl Protestant or Catholic, it did not matter. A girl just needed to be something.

Her skills as a seamstress were decent enough, but she often would miss appointments and deadlines because of drunkenness. When that happened, her only option was to go back to the streets and sell her body for a coin so that we might have a bit of bread for our supper.

The winters were the hardest. We had a tiny apartment that consisted of one room that acted as bedroom, kitchen, living room, and a small washroom with a chamber pot in an alcove that we curtained off with a bit of fabric. The whole place always smelled like emptiness felt.

Moeder and I would not bother with night gowns or any kind of sleepwear in those winter nights. We would go to bed fully dressed and huddled together on our one little mattress under the warmth and comfort of a thinning blanket. Moeder disliked wearing her bonnet in the house or anywhere that she did not feel obligated for reasons that she described as feelings of confinement that turned into headaches. I, on the other hand, would wear mine to bed during those brutal winter nights in an effort to warm my ears while I slept.

I hated winters. We always had less of everything. Less food, less money, less comfort. Money for coal or wood to burn was never available, so we slept with the chill biting us to our very bones. The warmest part was Moeder's warm body wrapped around mine. She used to cup herself around me and wrap me in her arms against the chill. I was always grateful for that. She was the only thing in the room that did not feel empty and cold.

Chapter Two

The discomfort was at its peak when Sien brought the men she catered to home for their exchange. Luckily, this always occurred before bedtime, so the awkwardness of being roused from my bed was never an issue. This act of barbarism had a routine. When I heard the tone of two voices, one male and one my moeder's, outside my door, I was to make for the curtained washroom before they entered the apartment. Once behind the ratted curtain, I had to face the wash basin and close my ears to block out the grunts and desperate motions of what was taking place on the mattress that I slept on when the event was done. I always shut my eyes and ears to the deeds in our room, but I heard them anyway.

The men knew I was there. How could they not? Most knew Sien and knew she had a daughter. She had developed a reputation around The Hague. Plus, it was not difficult to spot my shoes under the tattered curtain that covered the alcove. However, it was another matter entirely for them to actually look into my eyes.

Most men looked instantly remorseful and small when I was not able to get to the alcove in time and they came face to face with the possible results of the action for which they were about to pay. In those times, I was to politely curtsy, duck my head, and escape to the alcove as quickly as I could manage.

Some men lost their zeal and left the apartment to go home. I imagined that they ran home to whatever daughter or sister my face had just reminded them. Most were able to continue with their plan after only a small amount of coaxing from Sien. She often told them that I was half deaf, and when I plugged my ears, I could hear nothing at all. A little liquor and a few small lies paved the way. Of course, the truth was that I heard everything.

It was in January of 1882, the year that I was seven years old, when the change of my lifetime occurred. It was a particularly difficult winter because Sien was again pregnant but only so much that she was barely showing. The man who fathered the child was a man who had become a regular client of Sien's, but when she broke the news to him that she was to have his child, he left the city to live with relatives abroad. He gave her a few coins for her trouble and apologized before he departed. He was not a bad man, just a weak man, and she harbored no ill feelings for him.

The baby he left behind was an issue though, and, by that January, food was even scarcer than it had been before. My grandmother had brought us a few items she could spare, but her husband had died some years before and her charwoman pay could only afford her so much.

That January seemed colder than ones past. I was curled in a ball trying to stay warm on our mattress one evening when I heard a male and female voice outside the door of our apartment. I grumbled out of tiredness and exasperation. My stomach echoed the grumble with the call of emptiness as I rose from the mattress and made my way silently to the alcove. I knew Sien had gone out to try to find "business," as she called it, that evening, but I had thought that it would be for naught. The night was especially cold, and most people would not be roaming the streets when it was that frigid. However, time was running out for Sien. The more pregnant she looked, the less "business" she would attract. We had already gone two days without eating.

I had made it behind the curtain just in time before the door opened. Heavy footfalls entered the small apartment. I sat on the floor and slumped against the wall waiting for this all to be over so that I could go back to bed. It was cold, and I tensed against the inevitable shivering that I knew was to come. I began to allow my mind to wander as it did to tune out the noises around me when I heard Moeder say my name.

"Maria?"

No. Not only was she saying my name, she was calling to me. I was perplexed. Was she really calling me to come out? I was nervous and desperate not to make a mistake, so I waited and listened. If I came out too soon, there was a good chance I would ruin the deal. Then, there would surely be no food. It was silent for a while and then I heard it again.

"Maria? Come out please."

I stood up timidly and peeked out from around the curtain to see Moeder standing there beckoning to me, her hand outstretched. A man stood next to her looking at me. I instantly felt like I had made a mistake, and I almost ran back behind the curtain.

"Come out, dear. There is someone I want you to meet."

Confusion swirled in my young mind. Moeder had always told me how important my invisibility had to be when she brought "business" home, and now, I was to meet one of these men? I did not want to meet him. Shyness flooded my cheeks and face. I was unaccustomed to experiencing shyness, but my cheeks were flushed all the same.

"Come forth child. Do not shy away. We both know you are not meek," she said coaxingly.

I walked out of the alcove and approached the two of them standing side by side. The man was not tall in the least. He had the face of someone about the age of my moeder, maybe younger. The clothes he wore were poor in appearance but clean and well mended. His skin was fair. His hair was a strawberry blond color and was cut fairly close to his head all around. He had a short, manicured beard of a lighter color. His eyebrows were nearly the same color as his skin and therefore seemed almost invisible at first, but when I saw them knit in an expression of kindness, I relaxed a little.

It was his eyes that really struck me. They were a grey blue, not a terribly uncommon color in the The Hague, but the way the blue cast itself around pushing at the black of his pupils and reflecting the little bit of lamp light in the apartment was remarkable. The contrast of somber grey and vibrant blue gave even the most commonplace of his glances great depth of emotion.

Only as an adult remembering this moment can I glean all of this meaning and articulate it. At the time, all I could understand about his gaze was that his eyes could somehow appear somber, kind, and intensely understanding all at the same time. It struck me as remarkable.

"Maria, I would like to introduce you to Mr. Vincent Van Gogh."

Chapter Three

"Maria Hoornik," I replied extending my timid child's hand to the fair haired man. He smiled softly and took my hand in his in a gesture of greeting. His hands were rough and cold. They almost felt a little oily. I thought to myself how strange oily hands in the winter were.

"It is a pleasure to meet you, Maria," he said as he released my hand looking over to Sien with an expectancy I did not understand.

"So, where would you like me to be?" asked Sien gesturing around the room.

"Perhaps by the stove for your own warmth and comfort," he remarked with a light smile.

"Alright," she said as she began to move across the room to our stove which provided very little heat due to its lack of use. "Maria, please light the other lamps so that we may have more light."

I did as I was told all the while wondering at the expense and what was happening here? I was never involved in Moeder's "business," and this whole interaction frightened and confused me. While I was lighting the last lamp, Vincent came over to me and offered a good bit of bread with a little cheese smeared on it. My eyes grew wide as I took it from him. I tried to not to show how desperately I wanted to devour the entire thing right then.

"There you are. That's your payment for being my helper this evening," he said with a satisfied smile. "Perhaps you will be a part of my studies, too."

I froze. What were studies? Is that what he called what he was going to do with Sien? He would want to do those things to me? I was a young girl, too young for such things, but I knew that there were men who enjoyed despicable acts with children. Poor children knew such things. Moeder would never allow that. Even so, fear coursed through my body and infected my face.

"Do not fret so, child. Tonight, you are only my assistant," he said sweetly while patting the top of my head. "Now, go and fetch my satchel. Then, you may eat your bread."

He walked calmly over toward where my mother had positioned herself near the now lit stove and pulled a chair around to face her. I was not sure what "an assistant" meant, but as long as I was not the focus of his attention tonight, I knew that I would be safe enough. I just hoped that I was not made to watch.

I retrieved his satchel and brought it over to him. Something rattled around inside the bag that was unidentifiable to me. He bade me to sit next to his chair and eat my dinner as he posed Moeder like a doll on the floor. I ate and tried not to make a sound.

He signaled her to move her face this way and that or to move her legs forward and back until the position was to his liking. When he had gotten the pose correct, he looked down at his satchel next to me and removed some paper and a thin wooden board. He then extricated a smaller wooden box full of the rattling noise I had heard earlier. When opened, the box contained lots of pieces of black bits. The entire inside was covered in a fine black soot and the black bits of rock were what had clattered around inside.

"Now, what I need from you, young Miss Maria, is to open this box and hold it out to me whenever I reach down for a new piece of charcoal. Would you do that?"

I nodded. It seemed to be a harmless request, but I did not comprehend these bits of "charcoal" as he called them. He laid the paper on the board and began to draw with the black rock in his hand. His face, knitted with concentration, seemed to focus intently on Sien as he drew on his paper. It was not long before I could recognize the point of her nose and the line of hair in his handiwork. He was drawing her. He was paying her to sit still for him so he could draw her.

"Mr. Van Gogh is an artist, Maria," Sien explained while she sat still on the floor. "I am posing as his model."

An artist? I knew artists. Well, that statement was not honest. I had seen paintings a few times in the windows of fine gallery shops during our walks around the city. When there had been women depicted in those paintings, they were lovely, rose-cheeked beauties. They wore fine clothes and had a healthy appearance full of fleshy waists and round bosoms. They were not Sien.

My moeder was ugly. My honesty had no ill meaning when it came to my moeder because she knew she was ugly. She was thin and gaunt with stringy hair and a large, pointed nose that did not help with her sorrowful demeanor. Unless she took the energy to smile, which she rarely did, she had the general disposition of sourness. The fact that she smiled at me now was probably due to the fact that we were eating and that she did not have to take anyone to bed.

I thought about Mr. Vincent Van Gogh and his choice of models, and I could not help but judge that he must not be a very good artist to choose such an ugly model. How would his drawings and paintings ever be beautiful if his model was so far from beautiful? Either this man was a very bad artist or a really strange person. Perhaps he was both.

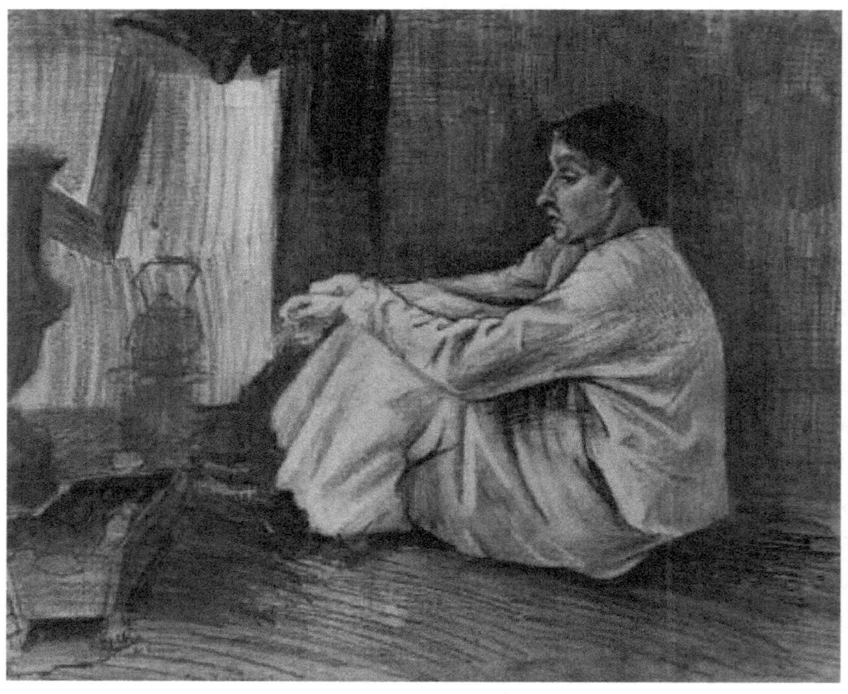

Chapter Four

I did pose for his studies soon after, and I was a far better model than Moeder because I could sit very still with little twitching. Mr. Van Gogh joked with Moeder and me that he had assumed the child would be the difficult model about moving, but it was the other way around. I had grown accustomed to sitting quite still and making as little noise as possible while Sien had the quavering hand of the long-time drunk. When she was more sober, she made an excellent model, and Mr. Van Gogh praised her thoroughly to encourage her toward longer periods of sobriety. I could tell that she responded to this praise. A soul hungers for the praise of a kind person, and Sien thrived and became more and more sober to please him with her stillness.

A strange man he was. He said that he had once wanted to be a priest, and I thought that perhaps his brief study of the bible might be the reason for his calm hand and kind words to someone like Moeder. He soon corrected me when I said as much in passing.

"No, my dear Maria. On the contrary, they thought me to be too much on the sympathetic side of paupers and beggars. I tried to live among them in squalor to truly experience their plight. I thought that if I understood their true lives, I might better my preaching to them."

"Was that not honorable?"

Actually, I thought it sounded perfectly awful. I was a poor child, but I always had a roof and walls to shield me from the cold. Why would anyone choose to live in muck and filth if it was not necessary?

"Apparently, my superiors thought not. They said that it was unseemly that a clergyman degrade himself so. How would sheep be able to look up to a shepherd who knelt just as low as they? I decided that the seminary life perhaps was not for me and that the artist's life would allow me the freedom to truly study my fellow man in all his forms."

I understood his meaning because the church people in our city always looked scornfully at Moeder and me on the few occasions we tried to attend their services. After a little internal debate, I decidedly dubbed Mr. Van Gogh to be a good person. He and I were both quiet people, and neither of us liked to waste words that were unnecessary. When I told him that I thought him to be good man, he smiled at the interruption to our comfortable silence.

"Were you so afraid that I was not a good person?"

"I did not know," I said.

We were cleaning up after a modeling session in the small apartment. Sien had taken a few coins and left to purchase some food for dinner. I had watched her as she dressed herself. After Mr. Van Gogh had declared the drawing complete, she had a slight smile on her face at the knowledge that we would eat tonight without the worry of her walking the streets in the cold again. He had asked her to pose nude this time. It was a sight that did not shock me. I had seen my moeder nude before, and the act of his drawing her motionless body seemed more and more natural to me.

"You did not trust me?"

He did not seem hurt; just honest. We were both plain people.

"I was not sure about you," I responded equally as honest.

"But you know now that I am no devil?"

"Yes."

"How do you know?"

"I just do."

"I could be hiding something," he prompted.

"I do not believe so," I retorted.

He eyed me not in a suspicious way but in the manner of a man trying to discern the meaning of a complex puzzle. Many of the people who took the time to speak to me looked at me like that eventually, as if I were some sort of enigma. What they did not understand was that there truly was no secret to me. Honesty was my game.

"How do you know I will not harm you or your Moeder?"

"If you wanted to hurt us, you would have by now. There is nothing to gain from feeding a starving woman and girl with no defenses and then turning the tables to harm them. That would be an idiot action, and you do not seem like an idiot to me."

He stared at me in that way again and was quiet for a moment.

"You have seen much for your age, have you not, Maria?"

"I suppose."

"You speak well for a girl your age."

"I listen to people, Mr. Van Gogh."

"Please, I thought that we had become friends now."

I thought about that statement. Were we friends? At that point, he had been at our home almost every day for two weeks. I had both posed for his drawings and discussed life with him. He had fed our hungry bellies with what money he possessed. I was not so naïve to think that he did not have the urges of a man, but the liberties he took with Sien seemed to be done when I was away. To the best of my knowledge, Sien did not seem to mind like she had with the strangers she brought in the house for only one night. In fact, several times I had entered the apartment under the accompanied arm of my Oma to find Mr. Van Gogh dressing and Sien whistling happily in her dressing gown. Her cheeks shone like roses in a way I had not seen in years.

I thought about my full belly, Sien's rosy visage, and the politeness that this odd fellow bestowed on me and my family. There were no falsities of which I knew. He knew Moeder's profession and her weakness for liquor, and yet, he came to us still with kind words and a caring heart. Was he my friend?

"Yes. We are friends, Mr. Van Gogh," I stated after my silent deliberation.

"Then you must call me Vincent," he said with a smile.

Despite myself, I smiled back at the extremely odd man.

<h1 style="text-align:center">Chapter Five</h1>

It was a week later when Vincent asked Moeder and me to move into his apartment to live with him. Well, he asked Moeder and not me, and she came rushing into the apartment to tell me in such a state that I thought that her body might give this baby up for the grave as well. She calmed enough to breathe the words out in gasps rather than speaking them.

"Vincent wants us to live with him."

"What?"

"You heard me, child. I know that you are not deaf."

"When we will move?"

"As soon as possible! Oh Maria, it is not terribly large a space, but it is bigger than this. I will have a bed to share with him, and you will have this one completely to yourself. Is this not exciting?"

"Yes," I answered unsure how to feel about this change of events.

"Oh, be excited! We will starve no more! Vincent wishes us to be a family and live together as such."

"Has he proposed marriage?"

"In good time, darling daughter. Always the practical with you, never the spontaneity! I named you properly for you are so much the copy of my moeder. But now, do not be my moeder! Be my daughter, and embrace me!"

She was excited, and I had to admit that it was infectious. I wrapped my arms around her, and she squeezed me until I grunted a little. We both giggled and smiled. Suddenly, her face grew grave, and she took my face in her rough hands. Her gaze was as piercing as her mood was fickle.

"You must promise me something, my Maria, in order to keep the happiness in our new family," she said urgently.

"What is it that I must promise?"

"You must promise to never tell Vincent about the babies."

"Babies?"

"The babies that I have lost. He is a religious and devout man, who may want his own children some day, and if he hears this news, he may believe me unfit to bear him children some day."

"But you had me, and he knows that you are pregnant now."

"Yes. I want to leave nothing to chance. Once he sees the wonderful mother that I am with you and with the new baby, he will have no doubts about marriage or children. I just do not want to frighten him away with that history."

I eyed her skeptically. She knew how much I hated lying.

"It is not a lie," she began, knowing my feelings all too well. "It is just not telling Vincent everything just now. I will disclose all later after the baby is born, and there is a marriage."

My face did not alter in its expression, so she pressed further.

"Please, Maria. Do you not like Vincent?"

"No, I like him."

"Do you not want to live with him and have a real family?"

I took a moment to ponder that.

"I would like that."

"Then promise me," she begged.

I hesitated and thought about my new friend. The past weeks had been pleasant despite the winter air. I remembered how much more that cold air would bite when I did not have a full belly to keep me comfortable.

"I promise."

*　　　　*　　　　*

We didn't have much to pack and move to the new apartment, and I was happy to see that Vincent's apartment was not only a little larger than ours had been but it was a great deal closer to my Oma's house. I could now feasibly walk there by myself if I wished to visit her.

His apartment boasted a large bedroom that was meant for Sien and him to share. The kitchen was adequate and opened to a small sitting room. Next to the kitchen was a crawl space pantry that made an excellent room for me. The mattress fit into the space just so, and I was elated to have my very own door. The furniture in the apartment was sparse but sturdy, and the stove worked better than ours ever had. It was not until Vincent showed me his studio that I was truly impressed.

It was an attached room that was papered much the same way as the rest of the apartment. Yet, this room felt so much more alive. The life came from the myriad of prints posted about the walls. Beautiful paintings and drawings littered the space like magic spells. There were so many that I could barely tell what the original wall paper of the room had been.

I looked in a dazed way about the room at the richness of the images. Vincent began pointing out several of his favorite prints to me while discussing their merits. He referred to prints and said names like Rembrandt and Delacroix. He spoke of these names like I should already know who these men were and the significance of their magical paintings. I refused to give away my ignorance. If my friend Vincent thought I should know them, then I would learn of them. I did not know why at the time, but I wanted desperately for Vincent to think me as intelligent and fascinating as he did these men.

He turned around to show me his writing desk. Stacked on shelves behind the desk were rows of books, paper, ink, and various art supplies. I mulled over the items in front of me, wanting to ask a thousand questions but not daring to venture even one. My careful attention landed on a small blue book next to some parchment. It stood out from the other possessions, and I allowed my eyes to roost there longer. When I looked closer, I noticed silvery letters impressed into a blue hard cover. I knew my letters, but I was completely ignorant as to what the letters said or meant. Vincent noticed my interest in the book and came up behind me.

"That is one of my favorites too," he stated as though I not only knew what the title of this book was but had read it thoroughly.

It occurred to me as an adult looking back on this that Vincent was not as observant as I had credited him. How could a girl of my age and upbringing possibly been capable of reading? The absurdity of it. And how terrible the idea felt. I was ashamed that Vincent assumed so high a skill from me and I was not able to live up to his expectations. Absurd that I would have had anyone to teach me, and yet, he just assumed. Truly his childhood had been a very different one than mine.

Perhaps Vincent had tried to live in squalor to understand the paupers because his childhood was so different. Maybe the only way for him to understand the commoner was to live as such for a time. This was simply not something he understood as of yet. Either way, I swore I would never tell him the truth.

I decided on no response. As Moeder had explained before, silence is not a lie. I allowed Vincent to assume the best of me, and we moved on to a portion of the studio where his paintings and drawings were stacked and hung about the wall. He explained that these were studies and they should not be compared to the finished drawings of the masters I had just seen. He was still learning. After I had examined them in their entirety with a careful eye, I stepped back next to Vincent to indicate that my evaluation was finished.

"Is there anything here you see that pleases you? Is there anything that you like?"

"Not really," I answered bluntly. As I said, I am an honest woman, and I was an honest girl.

A moment of tentative silence fell. Then, Vincent burst forth with exuberant laughter. I had seen bigger laughs from other men in the past, but never had I seen such a laugh come from Vincent.

"Well! You are my official art critic then, Miss Maria! There is no contest."

He patted me on the back as his laughter began to fade. I could not help but smile at the absurdity of the two of us.

Chapter Six

Life for us in that apartment became routine easier and faster than I had anticipated it would. The ease at which Moeder and I adjusted from our lives of poverty and the late night perversions of "business" to one of relative domestic comfort astounded even my child's mind. Granted our bellies were not full of the finest smoked meats and cheeses, but at least they were filled. Who was I to turn away soft bread?

The ease of this new life was also accompanied by a great amount of politeness that seemed strange to me given the fact that we all lived together under one roof. Sien and Vincent regarded each other with polite refrain, which I thought especially odd since they shared a bed with one another. He would not even call her Sien but addressed her as Clasina. It sounded foreign to both of our ears.

My Oma always said that I had a look of quiet scorn on my face, but I remember trying very hard to be agreeable in the beginning of our transition. I knew Moeder had her hopes of marrying Vincent, and, with so many indiscretions on her back, I wished to not add myself as another to burden. A scornful child, even a quiet one, was not a happy addition to any home.

Vincent, too, was silent, but I believed that to be his nature. I learned quickly that he was a devout man despite his dealings with Sien, and I thought that perhaps it was his religion that caused his quiet manner. His temperament fluctuated with the slightest word. He brooded from time to time, and I had a difficult time of it determining a bad mood on his brow from the intense focus over a drawing. Both visages appeared to be sour in attitude. I avoided him in either situation in an effort to not cross him if I guessed incorrectly.

It was a quiet and cold evening when I awoke to hear the sounds of sobbing from the direction of Vincent's studio. I rose from my bed warily, for the sound of a man weeping was not one I was accustomed to hearing. It wasn't uncommon to see homeless beggars sob on the streets during a cold evening all bundled in rags, but to hear a fed man do so in the comfort of a home seemed out of place. I stood and walked barefooted towards the studio despite the nipping cold of the night. I wished to not make the noise my shoes made on the hard floor and startle Vincent. When I opened the door that led to the studio, the hinge creaked and gave me away instantly despite my efforts at silence.

Vincent did not jump or startle very noticeably. He merely wiped his wet eyes with his sleeve and said, "You are very quiet, little Maria. Had the door not given you away, I would have not known you were there. Maybe I should call you Little Mouse."

He beckoned me closer and laughed a little at the disgusted look that crossed my face at the thought of my new name. I obeyed all the same and crossed the room to him.

"You do not like Little Mouse?"

"No, I do not like mice. They are vile and leave their droppings wherever they eat. They are pests."

He laughed again.

"I will not argue with you on that point. Perhaps a cat? A mouse would not have been able to move that big door, but a cat could do the job. Besides, you are scornful like a cat, and I think you not as meek as a mouse. I could call you Little Cat."

"Is not a little cat a kitten?"

"Yes, you are right, but that does not suit you, Maria. Even though you are a child, it is hard for me to see you as such, and a kitten is a child cat. No, I think Little Cat is perfect for you."

Despite myself, I smiled at the name Little Cat, and then quickly remembered why I had come to him in the first place. He had been sobbing.

"I heard you and thought you might be hurt. Are you well, Vincent?"

He smiled again through eyes glistening wet with recent tears.

"Yes, my Little Cat, I am fine. Just weeping as men are not meant to and over a woman no less."

He was sitting in his chair by his writing desk and looking at one of his portraits that he had drawn of Sien sitting in her favorite sewing chair.

"Moeder? Why do you cry over her? Did she do something terrible?"

Awful thoughts of Moeder back on the streets prostituting came to mind. It was true that we did not have much money with Vincent, but surely she would not do such a thing.

"No Little Cat, I am thinking of Klee."

"Klee?"

He put away his smile as he looked into the candle.

"Klee is my cousin, and I was in love with her. She is the reason why I am here now. She refused me and broke my heart. I remember after she refused me, I stood in front of her and her father and said that I would hold my hand over this candle's flame for as long as it took for her to love me in return."

As a child, this statement had confused me. I focused mainly on the pain of holding your hand over a flame for any amount of time. As an adult looking back at this conversation, I understand the amount of depth of emotional need Vincent was attempting to describe to me. I was a child, and it was safe for him to confide this to me because as a child, I was simple. I could not see the dangerous amount of need he had just described to me, and, therefore, my pity was superficial. All I saw was the pain of the fire, and I gave my friend the appropriately worried look he wanted.

"Did you burn yourself," I asked as I looked at his hands, scanning for a scar of some sort.

I had burned my leg once when I was little. I walked too close to the stove and burned the side of my leg. A discolored scar showed the remnants of the wound it had caused.

He laid the drawing down on the desk and showed me both hands unscathed.

"No, Little Cat, I did not. Her father blew the candle out before I could hold my hand there long enough to burn. He told me to stop acting this way and to leave. I did so and have been carrying the ghost of my love for Klee around like a shroud."

"Then why do you look at Moeder's portrait and think of Klee? Why do you weep here alone, Vincent?"

"Ah, that is because your moeder has saved me. The heartbreak of Klee killed my soul, and I had been walking about as a ghost walks about. Your moeder has resurrected me, and now, I live again."

"I do not understand."

"Little Cat, you know that I mean to marry your moeder, yes?"

"I thought you might, but I did not know."

"Yes, I do. Before you moved here, I told her, 'I am poor and no seducer. Do you think that you can put up with me? Otherwise, it must end now.' And to this, she replied, 'I will stay with you even though you be ever so poor.' To me, that will suffice as an engagement."

"Strange engagement," I said.

"Yes, but it is ours. She resurrected me, and I revived her. I am not sure if she has ever felt male kindness and love like mine before. It suits her. Do you not think she is looking well?"

"Better than I have ever seen her."

We looked together at the charcoal drawing of Moeder in the sewing chair.

"You drew her ugly," I said suddenly. "Your drawing is nice, but she is ugly in the picture."

"Sien is ugly," he responded in a truthful manner.

I flinched suddenly at his use of her short name. I had never heard him call her that before, and I wondered what had changed. I decided to go forth with our conversation as though he had not said the name while I had him talking.

"Yes, she is, but are you not supposed to draw her prettier so your art will be prettier? That is what I have seen other artists do in their pictures. They draw pretty women."

"Little Cat, I choose to draw people as they are and not as others would make them. Sien is ugly, and I draw her that way," he replied simply.

"Was Klee pretty?"

"No. She was beautiful. She was stunning."

"Then," I began in a confused tone, "Why do you love Moeder?"

"Because she understands sorrow like I do. She and I understand it like no one else I have ever known. We were meant to love one another. Her soul is not ugly."

A long silence passed between us as I tried to understand that last statement. Most of Vincent's words seemed absurd and strange to me, and yet, they made a sort of sense that only those who have suffered the indignities of a hard life can relate to. To live as an unwanted and ugly woman was sorrow, and I could see that point. However, the idea that such a trait would be so attractive to any man was beyond my realm of comprehension. Vincent must be odder than I had originally thought.

"Vincent," I said to finally break the silence, "Am I ugly like my moeder? In your drawings, I am not as ugly as she, but I wonder if I shall grow to be ugly like her."

He smiled at me.

"No, Little Cat, you are not ugly as long you do not scowl. When you scowl, you look just as your moeder does. However, when you smile, you are quite lovely."

I smiled despite myself. The involuntary reaction pushed my cheeks into my eyes in a pleasant way.

He pointed to my face and said, "See there, lovely."

Chapter Seven

It was weeks later when I found Vincent frantically tinkering about his studio. There were papers and drawings strewn about on the floor. Since the weather was beginning to warm, he milled about the room barefooted. He was muttering and working himself into a state while Moeder tried to calm him with gentle words.

"They all look wonderful to me, Vincent," she cooed at him.

"They are not. I need to showcase the best. Only the best will make an impression."

"Why do you not call for your artist friend, Mauve? You do value his opinion, do you not? He would be more helpful than I could be."

"No. I do not wish to seek his counsel."

"Why?"

"We quarreled," Vincent said shortly.

"Oh, yes. The plaster pieces," she said with an air of sarcasm in her voice.

Overall, our new lives with the painter had much improved, as had our spirits. However, with comfort in the new routine came the resurfacing of old habits. Bitterness was second nature to Sien, so the poison of it would often leak out when she had exhausted her patience. Their fighting halted when I came into the room in order to spare me their harsh words towards one another. I would often take full advantage of this fact and make it a point to walk into a room at the very hint of a bickering in order to quell an oncoming argument.

I thought this time would be no different, so I walked into the studio without a sound. I often preferred to make myself visibly known before any sound could be heard. It was a game that I liked to play with myself ever since Vincent named me Little Cat. I liked the idea of being stealthy like a cat.

However, this time they did not halt their conversation upon my arrival. They continued like I was not there.

"Plaster molds," corrected Vincent, irritated.

"Well, yes, molds then. Surely it is something that can be overlooked."

"No," said Vincent.

"But, Vincent, he is your friend."

"And an imbecile when it comes to plaster," he snorted.

They were still quarrelling even though I was standing there before them. This was disconcerting. I decided to make a small noise in case either of them had not seen me enter in all their frustration. I shuffled my foot, but they only stopped their conversation long enough to look at me for a second before they began again.

"I do not understand, Vincent. If your uncle wishes to see your work, is that not a good sign? He may commission you to do something for him."

"Yes Sien, but my uncle is not coming to look. He is sending his associate Weissenbruch to have a look at my work. My uncle is wary of traveling to this part of the city if it will be a waste of his time."

This last sentence he said with a long pause, as though he were searching for an appropriate way to say the thing. He looked less agitated and more guarded as Sien assessed his true meaning in her mind. I was fairly certain I knew what he meant as well.

"So, your uncle is too high of a man to come visit you in your whore's house," stated Sien very bluntly.

I flinched. Nothing good would come now.

"Sien, please."

"I suppose that I am of enough quality to pose for your art but not to visit and share an afternoon with."

"You know that I do not see you this way. My uncle is small minded, but he does hold a certain rank in the art society in this city. He must be catered to in order for me to have a chance here. He truly is a kind man in his heart. Once I can get him to come here, I am certain that he will regard you otherwise."

"And your friend, Mauve. Do you really not speak to him because of this plaster mold disagreement?"

"In the beginning, yes. It was a terrible quarrel."

"And now that time has passed and heads have cooled?"

Vincent looked down at the floor. That was answer enough. Sien looked angry and sad at the same time. I just felt angry.

"Perhaps you should just leave us, Vincent," she said angrily through tears that were forming in her eyes. "Your friends would come back to you if your whore and her daughter were not around."

He crossed the space between them to embrace her, but she pulled away and wept into her hands. Vincent put his hands on her shoulders and tried to console her with gentle whispers, but Sien cried further.

Panic overtook me. I could not bear to lose Vincent now. I knew what life would be like without him. It would be as it was before, late nights full of "business" and empty bellies in cold beds.

I frantically took to arranging the drawings he had strewn about the floor. Sien was wrong, they were not all wonderful. Some were terrible, and I carefully made a loose pile of the terrible ones. I laid out a few of the better ones in a line on the floor and stood back to examine my work. I rearranged them several times. This was definitely a good showing of his better work, but I would not have classified any of it as *good*. It needed a centerpiece; a piece that was borderline great to mask the mediocrity of the other pieces around it. After some thought, I knew exactly which one would suffice.

They did not notice me as I raced around the little studio digging through papers and files. Sien still sobbed and Vincent held her. They were too busy in their misery to notice me, and besides, I was playing my silent game. I was the Little Cat.

I breathed a sigh of relief when I found the piece that I was looking for. It was the best one I had seen him do of Moeder. She was nude and bent over herself, sitting on a stump on the floor. It was very simple and very ugly. Well, her body was ugly in the drawing. Her breasts sagged down, as did her pregnant belly. She hid her face in her arms, and her entire posture gave off the feeling of sadness.

The simple way he had drawn her was what I loved about this one. She looked almost pretty in how sad she was, and I liked that her face was hidden. I could imagine that the woman in the drawing would at any time look up with a truly beautiful face instead of one that matched her body. He had written the word SORROW on the bottom of the image, which I thought was unnecessary but he insisted upon it. To me, the whole picture said the word, but it was not an ugly addition.

I took the piece and walked over to the couple. I tugged on Vincent's shirt, and they both looked at me for the first time since I first entered the room. Sien's eyes were wet and blurry.

"None of these are great, but these on the floor are your best," I said as I pointed to the line of drawings on the floor.

Vincent and Sien just stared at me dumbfounded. I handed him the one of Moeder that said SORROW.

"This is your best one, Vincent. You should put this one in the middle and make sure he sees it. Maybe pin it a bit higher than the others."

Moeder looked at Vincent in an apologizing fashion. I supposed that she was shocked at my behavior and was worried that he would be offended. She had never seen Vincent and I discuss art before. I knew he would not be mad.

Vincent just smiled like I knew he would as he took the drawing from me. He patted my head gratefully.

"Thank you, Little Cat. I'll do just that."

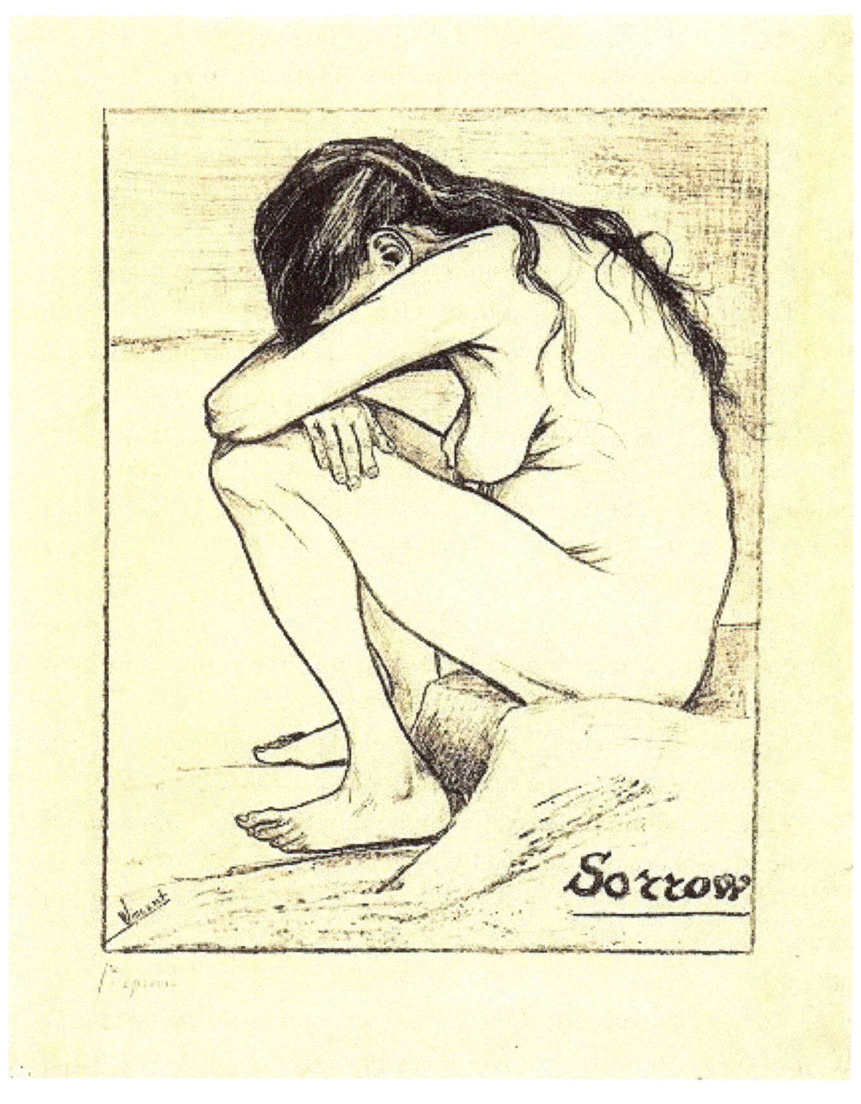

Sorrow

Chapter Eight

On the day that the man Weissenbruch was to come to the house, I was restless and full of anticipation. I only had three dresses that hung in my room, and only one was fit for accepting a visitor. It was a dark blue dress that my Oma had made for me, and I had tinkered with it endlessly the evening before in the hopes of eradicating all imperfections. I would show this man that we were not as low as he might think.

I practiced formal greetings in the bit of mirror we had in the washroom. I tried over and over again to curtsey the way I had seen in paintings, but the task was difficult in my wooden clogs. If I could only remain barefooted, I could accomplish the maneuver perfectly. With my shoes, it was impossible to be perfect. I stumbled a few times before I was able to make a gesture that I thought to be right enough for the occasion.

Vincent avoided me that morning, but I did not take offense. He was prone to mood swings, and the visit of such an important man obviously made him nervous. I left him alone to his sulking, which he tended to keep to his studio.

The odd thing was that Moeder was quiet and sulking as well. Even though she often brooded over nothing important at all, her demeanor this morning was hard to judge. I could not understand why I was the only one excited about this day. The very air about her made me nervous when I stepped into the kitchen.

"Good morning," I said lightly, testing the waters of her mood.

"Good morning, Maria," she said with nothing in her voice.

Her tone was not sharp, nor was it frustrated. It just was, like the nothingness of a dreamless sleep. I could feel the anxiety build up in my chest, but I chose not to show it.

6   "What time will the gentleman be here today?"

Sien turned to look at me with a sullen gaze.

"You look fine today, Maria. Too fine to go to the market with me."

She tried for a smile, but it hung strangely on her face. I felt a rock land in my stomach.

"The market?"

"I am afraid that you must change your dress. Your Oma will be terribly disappointed if you tore that dress. The market is too filthy a place for that. You must change into your gray dress. That will suit you better today."

"But, Moeder, the gentleman is coming today. You know this. I am dressed to help you receive him."

I could feel the childish tears begin to form in my eyes. They felt warm and completely unwelcomed. I blinked angrily to keep them at bay.

"Yes, Maria, the gentleman is coming today to look at Vincent's work. However, you and I will be busy at the market and will be unable to receive him."

I knew what this meant, and I knew now why Vincent was avoiding us this morning. We were not fit to receive his guest. He did not want this gentleman to judge his whore before he judged his artwork. The tears turned hot and angry in my eyes, and I scowled at the weakness in my moeder's helpless face.

"Now, Maria, do not look such. Vincent needs this visit to go well. It would be better if we were not here."

I said nothing and stared hard at the floor trying to will the tears to retreat.

"He has managed a little extra money for us to take to the market to treat ourselves. We can get something sweet if you like."

She was trying to brighten the insult with a bribe.

"I do not like sweets."

"Well, we can get whatever you like. Look here," she said as she pulled a handful of coins from her pocket. "See this? See how generous Vincent was. He gave us this much to go treat ourselves."

I stormed back into my room and removed my finest dress. I replaced it with my gray one and tied my hair with a bonnet. When I returned to the kitchen, Sien stood there looking sullen. Her face fell further when she saw me in my new clothes.

"Let us be off, Moeder," I managed to say with little emotion. "Be sure to bring your parasol. The clouds look heavy."

Her mouth fell open in surprise, but she grabbed the parasol and followed me out of the front door. We said nothing more as there was nothing more to say. A whore and her daughter; we were fit to share a home but not fit enough to receive his visitor. The message was plain. What more was there to say?

We left our apartment and began the walk to the market. The clouds were indeed heavy, and they began to trickle light drops of rain on our heads. Sien opened the parasol and covered us as we walked, holding me tighter to her so that I would be protected from the weather. Her embrace tightened and began to feel like an apology.

Just before we turned on the street that would lead us to the market, I looked back at our home to see a carriage stop in front of our building. A large man in a tan suit emerged looking around him with interest. As he stepped from the carriage, it shifted with the sudden loss of his weight. Even the horse looked relieved. He gave his driver some orders that I could not hear.

When we turned, I could no longer see the man in the tan suit. I am not sure what I had expected. Jewels? A royal procession down the thoroughfare? My child's mind had pictured something much grander that would deem Moeder and me so unfit to receive him in our own home. The grandeur was lost to me, and I was all the bitterer for it as we trudged through the rain to the market.

"Does not look so fancy to me," I muttered to myself.

We did treat ourselves. Sien bought red apples and let me eat one while we walked from one vendor to the next. Such a luxury was this that I could not help but to brighten. The apple was sweet and the juice ran down my chin in a satisfying way. I wiped it off with my fingers and licked them to waste as little juice as possible.

We also bought soft bread, eggs, coffee, milk, and cheese. The cheese was the softest kind that I enjoyed the most. I knew Vincent was paying for our absence, and I was planning on making sure he paid dearly. The eggs and milk were an extra extravagance for us.

When we reached the smoked meat vendor, my mouth instinctively began to water despite the whole apple in my stomach. I loved meat, and it was so rare that I had it with any meal. Sien saw my face as we neared the vendor and dutifully spent the remainder of our money on some smoked pork and bacon. Tonight we would have a handsome dinner.

When we returned home, Vincent was standing anxiously by the door. I was determined to remain angry with him, but his ecstatic smile upon viewing us was infectious. How could you remain cross with someone so happy?

The visit had gone well and the man in the tan suit was going to go back to Vincent's uncle suggesting he come and see his nephew's work himself. Vincent was overjoyed, and we were elated for him. We made our handsome dinner and ate like kings. We were royalty that evening. Even though I too was wrapped up in the joy of the evening, something inside me did not let me forget the injustice I had suffered in order to make this celebration possible. It stuck to my very skin, and I left it there to examine over and over again later.

Chapter Nine

C.M. was the name Vincent called his uncle. It was a strange thing to call a person of your own blood, but who was I to judge such customs? What I did judge was that Moeder and I were asked yet again to leave while this C.M. came to view Vincent's artwork personally. This time, however, the injustice was disguised as a visit to my Oma's house so Sien could properly be examined by a doctor. A doctor visiting the home of a sinful couple, especially when the woman was carrying another man's child, was absolutely out of the question in polite society.

This did make sense to me. A visit to Oma's house would be more proper for the doctor, but I knew that this was all a ruse to usher us out of the house before the infamous uncle arrived. Moeder knew it as well but held her face together to try to keep me calm.

A little cat I was not that morning. I stomped about the apartment and refused to speak. I made all of the noises that I knew Sien and Vincent hated the most to express my displeasure. When asked what was wrong, I huffed out a belly full of wind and shuffled something near me in an agitated state.

My plan worked. Vincent was frustrated and short with me due to his heightened anxiety. The calm he had wished to display was gone. I smiled when I saw how disheveled his hair had become after running his hand through it over and over again. He shot me angry glances as I banged about his studio.

"Maria, stop this now," he said through gritted teeth.

I continued my stomping louder.

"Maria. I need to relax before my uncle's visit. Stop this."

I stomped louder and kicked over a chair without speaking to him.

"Maria!"

He had grabbed my shoulder and physically stopped me.

"Stop this now! Do you not see that I need peace to prepare?"

I looked directly into his eyes, forbidding myself to cry. I scowled with all of my might hoping that I looked exceptionally ugly to him.

"It will not matter, Vincent. He won't like these anyway. You paint only ugly things, and your pictures are ugly."

This hurt him. I could see it in his eyes. I meant it to hurt. I was hurt and angry. I wished to make him hurt as well even if I did not believe my words. True, his pictures were not wonderful, but I did not think them ugly either. They were different, but I would not tell him that. I was angry, so my goal was to injure.

He demanded that Moeder take me away right then, and we left to make the short journey to my Oma's house. It was colder that day, so I huddled closer to Moeder despite my ever present anger.

"Maria," she said softly as it began to drizzle ever so slightly.

"Yes, Moeder?"

"You should not have said such things to Vincent. He has a sensitive soul, and such words wound him in ways that you cannot understand."

"He wounded me first."

"I know, but he is sorry for that."

"Did he say that he was sorry?"

"Well, no. He does not need to say such things. He is an artist. They are different that you or me. They contain feelings that our minds cannot fathom."

"If he did not say that he was sorry, how do you know that he feels sorry?"

"Well, he did say it to me last night."

"But he did not tell it to me. Vincent never told me that he was sorry, and if you are sorry for something, you should not continue to do it. This is the second time we have had to leave our home because he is embarrassed of us."

"This is only business. Vincent is not ashamed or embarrassed of us. It is only to help him get this commission."

"Well, he did not apologize to me," I pouted.

"He does not need to. You are a child, and he is your elder and your better. You will do as he says because he is our provider now. I will hear no more about this from you, Maria."

She was practically yelling by the time we reached Oma's home. In fact, Oma came out and met us in street having heard the tone in Moeder's voice from inside the house. She walked up to us with a look of warning on her round face. Oma was short and round in all of the places that Sien was pointed and thin. Sien had favored her father who had been made out of sharp angles as well.

"Screeching in my street? Have you gone mad? There are appearances to consider, Sien. Why do you carry on so in front of the child?"

"Oh, stuff the lecture, Moeder. You see what you can do with her. She talks back to her elders as though she were equal. And not just to me. Oh no, she has begun arguing with Vincent as well. No wonder he will not have us at home when his guests come to call."

She looked to me, and I knew what she was seeking. I would not give her the hurt she was trying pull from me. I stiffened my face and said nothing.

"I must lie down. I feel faint. Moeder, where is there silence in your home?"

Oma looked at Sien and then back to me.

"The parlor, Sien. It is quiet in the parlor. There is that nice chaise to recline in while you catch your breath and wait for the doctor."

Moeder stormed off towards house. Oma extended her hand to me knowing that I was too angry to accept forced touching at the moment. Appreciating her forethought, I took Oma's hand and followed her into her home. She led me to the kitchen where we sat at her table and drank milk together.

I loved my Oma. Out of everyone, she understood me the best. We thought alike. I admired the stubborn strength she carried with her. I thanked God regularly that I was named for her. It was truly some sort of blessing.

"So, what has happened, child? Why have you vexed your moeder so?"

"Vincent made us leave again. He made us come here so we would not embarrass him in front of his patrons."

She nodded in that solemn way she did when she was reading me. No one could read me like her.

"And you think it is because of you?"

"Yes, but mainly no."

"Well, which one is it? Yes or no?"

"He makes us leave because of Moeder. It is all because she is a…"

Just then, a knock at the door interrupted me. Oma commanded me to stay while she ushered the doctor in through the door with warm greetings.

"She is in the parlor. I will stay here with the child while you conduct your examination."

He nodded to her, and she returned the nod. He disappeared around the corner, and Oma returned to her place beside me.

"She is not that type of woman anymore child, and you know that to be the truth."

"But the fact that she used to be is the reason the men will not come to the apartment if we are there. I am angry with Vincent for not being stronger and defending us."

"Why would he? Has he known you for so very long?"

"No, but I help him."

"Oh?"

"I pose for him, and I help to select the proper drawings to show. He is not very good at that, so he asks for my advice. It does not seem fair that I am not there to help."

"Listen child, Vincent is a grown man and does not need your help. You are but a child, and while I am glad that he seems to be kind to you and Sien, never forget your place. Your moeder's place is that of a disgraced woman. She shall always carry that brand with her because she is good for little else. I know my daughter and her limitations. The men do not wish to be entertained at your apartment because of her. You have the unfortunate luck of being her daughter, so where she goes, you go. This disgrace you feel is not your own. It is hers."

"Am I disgraced?"

"Not yet, but if you go down her path you will be. You have the mind to raise your station from this. I know this about you. Your mind is quick."

I smiled at the compliment.

"Do not smile so, child. Your tongue is even quicker, and you have already begun to read the faults in people. You are using that talent to inflict pain and suffering. That is a childish game you play. I will not have you do as such again, especially to your moeder. She is a frail beast. She is not like you and me. Now, nod so that I know you are agreeing with me."

I nodded with all of the guilt I was feeling.

"As for this Vincent, I am wary of a man who lives on income attained from the charity of his family. However, as long as he is kind and you and Sien are fed, I have no objections. Learn your boundaries with him as well. He is your elder. You should not speak out to him."

I nodded again. I always admired the fact that Oma was an honest woman like me. It was difficult to disagree with someone like that.

The doctor came into the room and looked at us, first to me and then to Oma. His face was solemn.

"Mrs. Hoornik, perhaps the child should leave the room while I deliver the results of my exam."

My tongue caught in my throat. Was Moeder ill? Was she to lose the baby? Another baby lost to the illness of beggary and prostitution? I felt a swell of regret for the terrible way I had conducted myself earlier.

"Now that you have frightened the child, you had better rectify this situation and quickly tell us both the prognosis, Doctor. Maria has heard far worse, I am certain."

The doctor stiffened and said, "Very well. Your daughter is healthy, though she could use more meat in her diet. More food in general would be beneficial. She will probably deliver her child in late July. I have recommended that she go to Leiden when the time comes."

"Thank you. Here is your pay."

I watched Oma drop a thin coin into his hand, and he turned to leave us. Before he vanished, he turned around and addressed her again after casting a glance at me.

"The child should not have to hear such things Mrs. Hoornik. It is not a topic for young ears."

She snorted at him angrily, and he hurried for the door.

Chapter Ten

The days progressed as Sien grew larger and larger with child. Everything warmed, and with the warmth of May came a feeling of renewed energy and spirit. The world seemed a brighter place than it had in the colder months. The birds sang outside our windows louder than before. The gravity of one's bulk felt lighter somehow.

At least this was how the month of May struck the spirits of the women in our house. I ran about the house twirling in the warm air, bareheaded as a street urchin, and Moeder practically glowed from the enhanced sunlight. Vincent, however, seemed immune to the affects of May. He moped about his studio most of the day grumbling about this or that. He complained of ailments that may or may not have been real. The man even took to sleeping on the sofa in his studio most nights due to his sudden illness that could not be named. It was almost as if he were a flower that only blossomed in the cold and the dank, only to wither and die at the first sight of light.

The beginning of May also marked the day I decided to investigate the origin of Vincent's money. The amount Moeder had in her pocket for groceries was growing smaller by the day. Being the child that I was, I had not questioned where his money had come from before, but now, I was growing ever more concerned. I never saw him do any work that might pay him a wage. The drawings C.M. commissioned him to do had not been completed yet, so the rest of the commission had yet to be paid to him. Where did he get this coin?

I watched him often, wasting away in the sunlight. At least, that is how I perceived him at the time. I noticed after a while that he would perk up considerably whenever the mail carrier had left a bundle upon our doorstep. He sometimes raced for the door, tearing open letters and reading the contents voraciously. I watched his face fall into renewed despair after emptying the coins into his lap. The want to learn to read grew every time I saw this. I wanted to know what the letters said.

One evening, after Sien and Vincent thought I had gone to sleep, I practiced my Little Cat sneaking around the apartment game. I overheard whispering in the kitchen, so I went to investigate.

"This is not enough to live, Vincent! What happened to the rest of the money from your parents?"

"They are not going to send me as much as they once did. They are angry with me for moving in to this place with you and Maria."

"They disapprove of your whore," Sien spat at him.

"Yes," he said plainly as he looked into her eyes.

Moeder said nothing and forced a few tears back behind her eyes. His admission had obviously not been anticipated.

"Sien, they do not know you as I know you. They do not know Maria. They cannot see the happy, loving family we have here. I have invited them to visit us so that they might see and understand what we have. I think that if I can get them to come for a visit, it will soften their disposition."

"If?"

"As of right now, they are unwilling. However, I do believe I can convince them with time. If they could only see us and the work I'm creating, I am confident that they will change their minds."

"And how long will that take? Look at this, Vincent," she said as she pulled out a loaf of black bread from her grocery sack. "This was all I could afford today. We have coffee, water and this loaf of stale black bread to feed us tomorrow. What shall we do?"

"Some people have less, my dear."

She glared angrily at him.

"Do not speak to me of less as though you were a holy man. I know what less is."

"I know Sien. I promise it will be better. I will convince them."

"And if you cannot? What then? How will we survive, this happy family of ours?"

"We will survive. I will be paid soon for these first drawings. With luck, I hope to get more commissions. Soon, we will not need assistance from my parents or my brother, Theo."

"Is Theo the only one who sends us money any longer?"

"No. My parents still send money, just not as much. They threaten to stop sending anything. But Theo is a true brother, and a man of great compassion. He would not do such a thing. We will be alright."

"What about your art supplies? We can stop buying so many and afford more food for us."

Vincent suddenly looked very dark and serious.

"I use everything I buy, Sien."

"Yes, but if you slowed down or used your materials more sparingly…"

"No," he snapped, stopping her in her tracks. "I need these to learn and to earn commission money for us. It is more important to me than food. I will be as frugal as I can, but I will not compromise my practice for a few more comforts."

"Comforts? I do not consider milk and decent bread a mere comfort."

"I said no, Sien."

He was unmoving. She sat still, angry and unwilling to further the conversation. I slipped back to my bedroom silently and tried to sleep, all the while listening for any murmurs to indicate the stalemate in the kitchen had resolved itself. I never heard another word from them that evening. I went to sleep dreaming of what this mysterious Theo must look like and hoping for soft bread for breakfast.

Chapter Eleven

"Be still, Sien! The slightest movement alters the light on your face."

Vincent was in a sour mood. The blackness of his temperament enveloped the studio and seeped into my skin. Moeder was not helping matters. She had been sneaking alcohol and was finding it difficult to be a still model even though he had let her sit on a basket instead of the floor this time. I sat on the floor next to her holding my knees to my chest as motionless as a stone.

"Ah, see how Maria is so perfectly still? I already have her roughed out here nicely. I need you to do as much. If she can do it, surely you can manage."

She glowered at him. "Perhaps if you let me actually sew instead of pantomime the act, it would seem more natural. I might actually finish this dress, and then I would be paid."

The tone in her voice was sharp. I hated when they fought this way. It was like dancing around a fire and tickling it with a branch. Any moment the fire would erupt and catch the branch ablaze. I wondered if he could smell the drink on her breath. I could, but I was sitting very close to her.

"Fine. Whatever helps you."

He went back to work scribbling furiously on his paper. Ten minutes later he rolled his eyes and hit his paper with the back of his hand.

"Sien, if you must move, at least keep your face still! How can I possibly get the curvature of your nose if you keep moving and changing the light on your face? This is impossible!"

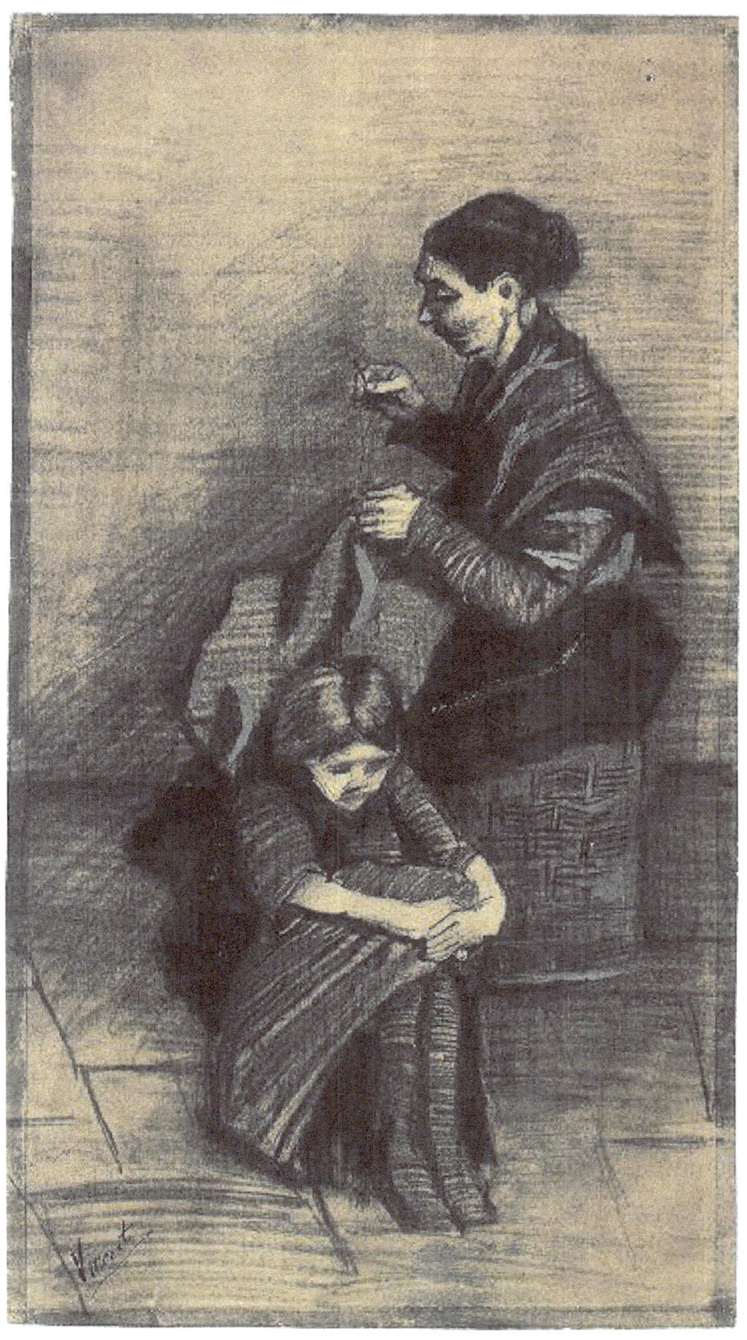

Moeder's features hardened as she stood suddenly flinging her sewing work to the floor. I was able to move just in time to slide out of the way.

"That is enough for today, Vincent. I am going to go rest now. This is all far too stressful, and you are the ugliest sort of creature right now!"

With that, she stormed out of the studio and slammed the bedroom door. Vincent stood and kicked away the stool he had been using. He went to the window with both hands on the sill and peered out angrily. I took a deep breath and exhaled it in frustration as I rose and walked over to him.

"You cannot do that to her," I said as I approached his hunched form.

"Not now, Maria."

"I mean it, Vincent. You will not get what you want from her that way."

"What do you know about it," he grumbled.

"I know her. If she's hungry, she steals drinks. If she steals drinks, she is a terrible model."

He looked down at me with a mix of surprise and anger.

"Yelling at her makes it worse. I do not know why you are so cross, but yelling will not get her to do what you want."

"So what does work? The all knowing Little Cat must know."

He was being sarcastic now. I hated when adults did that.

"Feed us!" I snapped at him.

He stopped short, and I saw him soften under my glare. Vincent slumped on the floor, and ran his hands through his hair.

"I am trying. I swear it. My uncle will be here this very evening to look over the drawings he commissioned from me. If he likes them, he will pay me the rest of the money."

"Then why are you so unhappy?"

"Because I cannot tell if they are good enough. The frustration is overwhelming me and making my face hot."

He rubbed his eyes violently and moved the motion to his hair. I patted his shoulder and made him look into my face.

"Will you show them to me?"

He let out a long sigh and stood up with a great deal of bluster. I watched him as he dragged out all twelve of the drawings his uncle had commissioned. He lined them up on the floor, and we looked down at them together.

"He asked for twelve drawings of The Hague," Vincent said as I walked around looking over the work.

I was silent for a while as I looked at everything. These were not very good. He was forever choosing ugly scenes to draw. Why did he always insist on drawing ugly things?

"Out with it, Little Cat," he said, frustrated.

I stepped over the group closest to me and looked up at his face.

"They are not very good, but they are not very bad either."

He sighed again and slumped into a nearby chair.

"Do you hate them all?"

"No. I think the one of Oma's neighborhood courtyard and the carpentry yard are the best. You should show those first and put them up the highest so your uncle can see them better."

He looked down at the floor and sulked. I stepped quietly over to him without getting close enough to touch.

"Maybe you should try to draw the pretty places in The Hague. It would make for prettier drawings."

I was trying to be helpful, but it seemed to frustrate him more.

"Not everything in this world is pretty," he snapped.

"No, but people like to think it is. They like to see pretty things on their walls."

"That is not what I draw, Maria. Not all drawings are pretty. Millet believed that the peasants were where you could find true artistic beauty, and I agree. I drew where the peasants roamed in The Hague and not the finery. Finery is false."

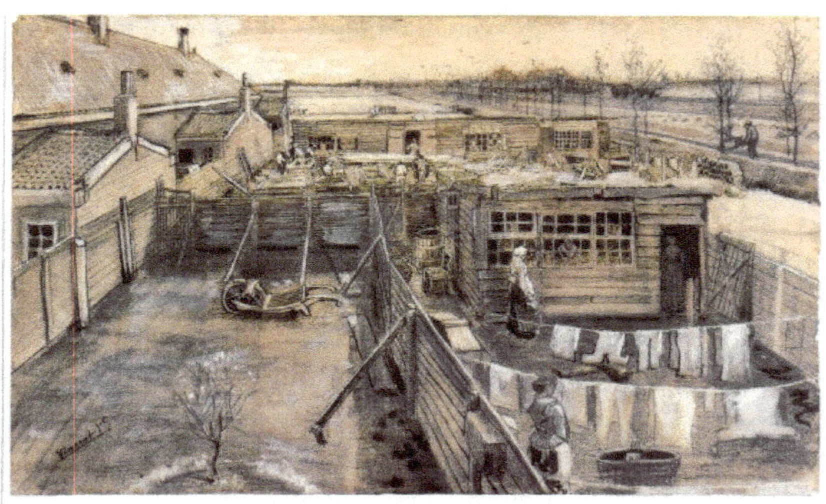

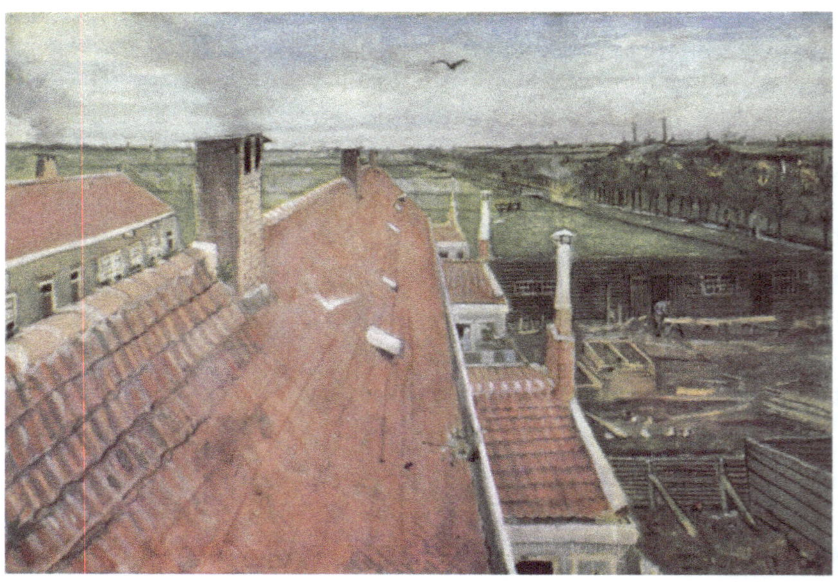

I had heard him speak of this Millet before, but I never dared to ask who the man was. Vincent acted as though I should know of him, so I played as though I did. I would never tell him when I did not know something. He might stop listening to my opinion.

"They are really not that bad, Vincent. If you were trying to draw the ugly things, you did that well."

I was trying to be soothing, so I put my hand on his shoulder. Another thought occurred to me while we existed together in that silence.

"Vincent," I began slowly, "Will Moeder and I have to leave when your uncle comes tonight?"

I felt his torso rise and fall under my small hand with a few deep breaths. He looked at me with a soften disposition.

"No, Little Cat, you may stay. Besides, I doubt I'll be able to convince Sien to go anywhere. I will let her rest in the bedroom."

Excitement filled my chest, and I smiled grandly at him.

"Be calm now. You cannot be visible when C.M. comes for his visit. You must be the very best Little Cat you can be. Stay unheard and unseen."

"Of course, I will," I said as I beamed up at him. I ran over to the drawings and began to rearrange them in a better order. I picked out my two favorites and pinned them on a board higher than the others.

"Be careful with those. Do not pierce the paper," Vincent instructed.

I knew better than that, but I did not tell him so. I handled every drawing with great care in anticipation for the mysterious man's arrival while Vincent sulked and worried by the window.

*   *   *

The moment arrived. I ran to hide myself in my small room when I heard the rapping on the door. I peered out of a split in the door to see Vincent straightening his clothes in front of the wash basin in the kitchen. He answered the door with a smile and welcomed his uncle into his home.

Moeder had not yet emerged from the bedroom, and I was fairly certain that she would not for the rest of the evening. For my part, I was to be the silent Little Cat that Vincent needed me to be. He was counting on me.

I watched C.M. walk into our kitchen. He was much taller than Vincent, and he wore a finer suit than most I had seen. He had cleanly cut hair and a slight belly that tugged at the waist of his pants. His face was shaven except for a manicured nest of beard that resided solely on his chin. The two men did not look related at all until I saw the man's eyes. He possessed those same large, sad eyes that Vincent had.

"Come this way, Uncle. The drawings you requested are in the studio."

The two men walked into the studio and shut the door behind them. This was my chance to prove what a good Little Cat I could be. I opened my door only enough for my body to manage through, and I walked very carefully through the kitchen and over to the studio door. Luckily, the floor was warm enough to not sting my bare feet. I made not a sound as I squatted down to peak through a slit in the studio door. It was time for the Little Cat to spy.

The men were looking at the drawings that I had set up so carefully. C.M. stood quiet for a long time as he surveyed the work. He stroked his whiskers while staring intently at each piece in kind. No words were exchanged for a long time. I could see Vincent shifting from foot to foot anxiously behind him.

"These are not what I was hoping for, Vincent," he finally said in gruff voice.

"What do you mean?"

"These look more like studies than final drawings. They lack a refined quality that my patrons desire."

"Oh, I see."

I saw Vincent try to not show his disappointment, but I felt it too. My shoulders slumped, and I fought back tears as my stomach rumbled unpleasantly from hunger. The sound was not loud enough for the men to hear, and the long silence in that uncomfortable studio continued uninterrupted for countless minutes.

"You look gaunt, Vincent."

"Uh, yes Uncle. I have been ill."

"Have you been eating enough?"

"There is not much appetite with this illness of mine."

"Have you been to a doctor?"

"No. I have been diligently trying to finish these for you. I'm sorry that they are not to your liking. Perhaps if you give me a little more time, I could improve on them."

"I see. To be frank, Vincent, there is not much to improve upon here."

C.M. looked them over again and stopped at the two that I posted higher than the rest. He stared intently at them for a few minutes.

"Well, perhaps these two. These are definitely your best drawings. They are actually quite nice."

I jumped a little inside of my body. The triumph of being proven correct was elevating. It felt like I might wet myself, so I squeezed my legs together to keep my water inside just in case.

"Thank you, Uncle."

"Yes, I think these show that you do have talent. We just need to get you to focus it a bit more. I will pay you the other half of the commission for these, and I will commission six more from you. However, the next six must have more detail. No more studies like these. Agreed?"

"Agreed. Thank you again, Uncle."

"No thanks, Vincent. Just please eat something. You look terrible. I'll pay you for the next drawings after I see them finished."

C.M. dropped some coins in Vincent's hand and began to roll up the drawings to take with him. I was so excited that I barely remembered to go back to my room and hide when the men exited the studio. I just barely shut my door in time before they came barreling into the kitchen.

They bid each other farewell as they both walked out of the front door. I had expected Vincent to come back in immediately and rush to tell me all about what happened, but he did not. I waited and watched the front door, but I saw no sign of him. I thought about going after him, but I was afraid of being seen by C.M. in the event that the two men were still talking outside. That would ruin everything.

I stayed in my room and laid my head on my pillow. Waiting was something that I hated to do, but what choice did I have? I waited and waited, jumping at every little noise. I imagined every creak was his footstep and every gust of wind was the door opening. Where could he possibly have gone? Why would he leave so suddenly? My young mind finally relented and fell asleep.

I awoke to someone whispering by my door.

"Little Cat? Are you awake, Little Cat?"

I rubbed the sleep from my eyes and opened the door to see Vincent sitting on the floor in the kitchen next to my door. He had two plates in his hands and a huge grin on his face. Happiness flooded the air around us.

"Where did you go?"

He put the plate in front of me without a word. His only communication was the smile he stretched from ear to ear. On the plate sat a large piece of fresh bread, a significant amount of cheese, and a small sausage link. The smell of the food was intoxicating and water filled my mouth. It had been a long time since I was confronted with such a bountiful meal.

"I apologize for not saying anything, but I wanted to go to the market before the stalls closed for the evening. I assume you heard everything that happened with my uncle? You are my partner Little Cat, so you get some of the reward."

My large grin gave away how happy I was. I reached for the bread and tore away a piece before a terrible thought entered my mind. I felt selfish.

"Vincent, what about Moeder?"

"What about her?"

"Should we not wake her too and share this with her?"

He gave me an affectionate look and patted me on the head.

"No, let us not wake Sien. She would not wish to be waked. I have saved some food for her to enjoy in the morning."

He leaned in closer and whispered as I imagined conspirators must whisper.

"Besides, tonight is for us. We are a team, you and I."

Vincent and I ate like kings on the floor that night, and we were happy with our small victory. We laughed and talked as though C.M. had actually liked the drawings he just bought from us. The next ones would be perfect. They would only get better and better from now on. It was our project, Vincent's and mine.

Chapter Twelve

Vincent's health deteriorated, yet he continued to slave away on his drawings. Moeder, too, started feeling worse. She was sick with pregnancy but somehow being close to Vincent made her worse. They were both pale and yellow around their eyes, and they dragged about the apartment like the dead walking. Their skin hung from their cheekbones, and their throats were raspy when they spoke. A walk from the one room to the next seemed to exhaust both of them beyond belief. I stayed a safe distance from them as it seemed every noise I made was met with irritated glares.

It finally came to pass that Theo had sent a little extra money to us. The idea was that Vincent was to use the money to enlist the aid of a physician to see to his illness. Instead, he used the money to take Sien to the dunes for a holiday.

"Fresh sea air is all the medicine we need," said Vincent one evening. "It is better than any hospital."

So the arrangements were made, and I was sent to stay with my Oma. Sien walked me through the streets of The Hague just before their departure on a Tuesday morning. The only downside to any visit with my Oma was the walk to her house. It was a blissfully short journey, but I had to pass the fishery drying house. The smell of salt and scales filled my nostrils with its foul odor, and I could not help but wretch every time I passed it. This time was no different, and I vomited behind a nearby shrub.

"Oh, come now, Maria. The last thing we need is another sick person. You will make me lose my stomach as well."

Moeder lifted me up, and I spit out the remainder in the grass. We hurried onward to Oma's apartment to escape the smell of fish and bile.

Sien did not stay there long. She waved away any offerings of food while holding a handkerchief to her mouth. For a moment, I thought she might vomit on the floor before she had to leave, but she seemed to compose herself. Moeder kissed me lightly on the forehead and bid us farewell. I watched the fragile thing disappear into the morning mist with feverish sweat on her brow.

"Eck, your moeder!" exclaimed Oma.

She slammed the door and made her way to the kitchen. Her house was warm and smelled like bread. My mouth watered given that I had just lost the contents of my stomach a few minutes before my arrival. Now that the fish smell was gone, I followed her with high hopes of bread and cheese. I was rewarded with both and a glass of milk. It had been days since milk had touched my lips, and I drank it greedily. Oma watched me and poured me another glass.

"It is just vanity thinking they know better than a doctor. It is plain as day that she holds the illness of a prostitute and he holds the illness of those who frequent them. No amount of fresh air can cure that."

I looked up at her with curiosity.

"You mean he is pregnant now too? That cannot happen."

She smiled at me across the table.

"No, my darling. Pregnancy is the sickness of lovers. What I am talking about is something I should not share with you. It is the folly of adults. Just know they have no one to blame but themselves. That is all."

Everything was so quiet in Oma's house. No one ever screamed. There were no drawings or prints of struggling farmers or gods on the walls. Even the cats declined to venture into her yard to conduct their screechy business with one another. I wondered if they were afraid of Oma. Sien seemed to be at times, although I did not know why. Oma's house was like herself, sturdy and quiet. I liked it there. I was never afraid.

I was there for days before my uncle came for a visit. I had not met him as I recalled, so I had no impression of the man to compare to in my memory. Knowing an uncle was a promising adventure.

"Maria, your Uncle Pieter is here."

I followed her voice to the parlor where my Oma stood next to a man who loomed over her. He was dressed in a fine suit, at least it looked fine to me. He removed his hat when I entered the room. His hair was dark, and his brow was full of bushiness. I recognized Sien's nose on his face.

"Hello, Maria," he said in a deep voice.

His smile and the sound of his voice stopped me in my place. His demeanor rang of sincerity, but there was something strange in it. Under his skin slithered a hidden thing. Even the very air around him felt unfamiliar and a little frightening. I was related to this man?

"Is she simple?" Pieter asked Oma.

"Of course not! Maria, come to your senses, child."

Her words snapped me back to life, and I regarded this man anew. Surely, I was acting foolish.

"Hello, Uncle."

He walked over to me and around me, investigating my appearance.

"She is bigger than I thought she would be."

"She is a good, strong girl," said Oma.

Something in her voice was different. She sounded almost afraid as well. No, she was not afraid. Oma was never really afraid of anything. It was more like trepidation.

"I have to say that she is prettier than Sien. I was worried that she would develop her moeder's nose."

I scowled up at him. He had that very nose. Who was he to judge?

"Ah, but she definitely has Sien's disposition!"

He laughed at his own joke, and I tensed my body. Something was odd about this man. I did not like him.

"Tell me Maria, have you begun to walk in your moeder's footsteps yet? Or rather, have you begun lie in them?"

He leaned down to better see my reaction. His face was full of cruel angles, and a smile wriggled across all of them. It was like a crack edging its way along the grooves of a rock. Everything seemed naturally cruel. My face grew hot and a ripple of energy flooded my chest. I wanted more than anything to take a kitchen knife to that awful face of his, but I settled on slapping him instead. It happened so fast that I barely knew what happened, and the sound of it reverberated throughout the room before I felt the sting on my hand. Pieter laughed in reaction.

"Pieter!" screamed Oma.

She ran over and hugged me to her skirts. I hugged her back and refused to break eye contact with him first. That would mean that he would have won, so I glared at him with all of the hate I could find. This man would not beat me.

"What is the matter with you, Pieter?"

He broke eye contact with me to look at her. I won.

"She is the one who slapped me, Moeder. Why do you not scold her?"

"Because you deserved that! What is wrong with you that you would say such a thing to a child?"

"Somehow, I do not think this one is much of a child," he looked down at me again like a man selecting a cut of meat.

I glared at him. My hands were fists at my side, and they shook with adrenaline.

"No, not much of a child at that."

"Get out! Maria is a child, and she is a good child. I will not have this in my house. Get out!"

"Yes, yes, Moeder, I will oblige you," he said in a singing way as he returned his hat to his head. "Give my love to Sien and the new little bastard she carries when you see her."

"I will not!" she yelled as she chased him out of the parlor. I heard the door slam behind male footsteps. The sound allowed me to relax my muscles. My fists relaxed, my face eased, and my body shook with the shock of it all. I sat on the floor and breathed the air of relief when Oma came back into the room.

"Come here, child," she said as opened her arms to me. I ran to her and fell into her embrace without hesitation, trembling like a newly hatched baby bird.

"I am so sorry, my darling girl. I am so sorry. I had no idea he would do that after knowing you only a few minutes."

I wept a little into her skirts, but only a little. The idea of him seeing us so upset by his words made me choke back the extra tears.

"Who was that? Why was he so cruel? What is wrong with him?"

"Oh, my Maria. That is your moeder's brother. I love him because as a moeder, I must, but he is not a whole man. He loves to inflict cruelty on women. God only knows what terrors he inflicts on that strange, young wife of his. She always seemed so pious, but one never knows."

"Why is he that way?"

"I do not know. He is missing parts of his soul. Where compassion should be lies the sin of vanity and pride. His ambition rules his life the way your moeder's sorrow rules hers. She and Pieter do not speak much, and she did not want you around him. He insisted on meeting you. I thought he would behave himself if I was there. I had no idea he would act this way."

"Does he treat boys the same way?"

"He does not seem to. I have combed through my memories to find a moment in his life that might have scarred him, but I have found none. Bless me, but I am afraid that he came from within me missing part of his soul. I must have witnessed some horror I do not remember when I carried him. Seeing terrible sights can steel that from a child."

She hugged me tighter, and I could not help but reflect on what kind of childhood my moeder must have had with a brother who was missing part of his soul.

Chapter Thirteen

We did not tell Moeder about Pieter's visit when she and Vincent returned from the dunes. Her face seemed so bright and full of rosy health. The last thing I wanted to do was dishearten her now that she was feeling better. However, Vincent's face showed none of the ruby glow that Sien's did. He looked just as gaunt as before, and he walked as little as possible. He suffered from fevers and bladder issues, and his insomnia was worse than ever.

Soon, even standing became difficult for him without aide, and when two letters filled with money came to our home on the same day, Sien saw it as a sign. They now had the money to send him to a hospital, and Vincent was too weak to refuse. He was quarantined and allowed no visitors for a time. Sien said that they would have to give him Quinine pills and injections for a while, but we would be able to visit him soon.

In the meantime, we feasted like rich women. Without Vincent's need to purchase art supplies, we had money to spare. We treated ourselves to meat and sugar. Sien glowed with her round belly, and she let me feel while the baby kicked inside her. Apparently, it liked meat as much as I did.

The day we were finally allowed to visit him was a warm, sunny day. We brought him a basket of treasures that included dried beef, bread, and cheese to be enjoyed, not to mention a bit of sugar we had saved for him to put in his coffee. Sien wore her nicest dress that would still fit her, and I mine. We skipped into the hospital with the warmest of intentions and spirits. The nurses stared at us cautiously as though we were insane people who might steal the patients' bedpans. I stuck my tongue out at one especially surly nurse as she passed us with a scowl on her face. Sien giggled with me as we passed through the door of Vincent's room, spirits running high with giddiness.

What we saw changed everything. Our faces fell, and our happy mood dropped through the floor below us. Vincent looked as though he might already be dead. His face was grey. His eyes were yellow around the rims. There were dark circles under his eyes and under his cheekbones. The life seemed to have vanished from his face. He had lost weight, and I could see his bones under his hospital shift. He moved slowly and with obvious pain. I must have been gawking because he addressed me first.

"Do I look that terrible, Little Cat? Your face tells me volumes."

"I am sorry."

"Are you?"

"Yes."

"Do not be so solemn, my girls. I am feeling better, I assure you."

He smiled weakly at us. It reminded me of a how a skeleton might smile at someone. I swallowed a lump in my throat that almost made me choke. I looked up at Moeder who was trying to mask her shock and not doing a good job of it either.

"Come now," he said and waved us closer. "I see a basket in your hands. Have my angels brought me something?"

Sien seemed to be stuck in place for a moment, unwilling to move closer to the skeleton that used to be Vincent. I grabbed her hand and the basket and dragged them both to his bedside.

"We have, Vincent. Look," I said trying to regain the fanciful air we had shared earlier.

I opened the basket to reveal the treats within. He made a great show of excitement but ate very little. We tried to converse while he sucked on little bits of sugar, but the look of him had shocked Sien to the point of silence. It was not long before a nurse came around and told us that our visit was at an end. Vincent would need more rest than a longer visit would allow.

"Farewell, my ladies," he said to us.

"We shall be back for another visit soon, Vincent," said Sien in a smaller voice than she actually possessed. She kissed his forehead lightly and left the room. When she reached for the door, I saw her hand shaking.

I sighed and started to follow her when his hand reached out and grabbed mine. His hands were large and dry compared to mine, but he held my hand with the strength of a toddler. The sheer gentleness of the envelopment stopped me more than anything else.

"Little Cat, wait for a moment. Whether you believe me or not, I am better than I was. I feel stronger and stronger every day. I will recover."

"I am glad, Vincent."

"The one I worry about is your moeder. She is nearly to her time, and she seemed very shocked by my appearance. I did not know that I looked so terrible until I saw her face."

I thought about what Oma had said about pregnant women seeing horrors while carrying their babies. The thought of Moeder's baby having a part of its soul stolen by seeing Vincent this way sent a jolt of electricity through my heart.

"You do look…terrible."

"Yes, but I *feel* better. I do not think that Sien believes me. Such a shock can harm a pregnant woman, especially if she believes that I may die of this."

"I will tell her. I will tell her that I spoke to you and that you are better."

"That will be a big help, but you must promise me more."

"What? Anything."

"Promise me that you will care for her. Watch after her and make sure she is well. Frightening things sometimes bring babies too soon. Promise me that you won't let her out of your sight, Little Cat."

"I promise, Vincent."

"Good. That is good. Now run and catch up to her. I must rest."

I ran out of his room and through the hospital corridors to catch up with my moeder. She would not leave my sight, even for a moment. I had promised Vincent.

Two nights later, I woke to the sound of screaming.

"Maria. Maria!"

Ever since Vincent's warning, I had been sleeping in Moeder's bed with her like we used to before Vincent came into our lives. I sat straight up in bed and looked around Sien's room with anxiety and fear in my chest. She was not in the room. I looked around the dark room and could not find her anywhere.

"Maria!"

The kitchen. The sound was coming from the kitchen. I sprang out of bed and ran into the kitchen. A single lamp was the only light in the room. That lamp was what illuminated the horror in front of me.

"Moeder?"

Sien was on her knees next to the table. She held herself up by clutching the table's surface with her arms. Her nightgown was wet from her waist down and there was a pool on the floor beneath her knees. The room smelled rusty and tangy like the butcher's stall at the market smelled. I noticed that much of the water on the floor was blood. Blood also stained her nightgown and hands. Her hair was matted about her face. When she looked through it at her bloody hands, she began to tremble and fell to the floor. I was stunned into motionless silence.

"Maria! The baby! It's coming early!"

She wailed in pain and clutched her belly. I ran to her not knowing what to do. I had been there when the other child had come, but I could not remember there being so much blood. It was everywhere. The red of the blood was black in the dark room and it saturated everything.

"Go! Maria, go to Oma's! Run to her! She will get the doctor."

I stood without thinking and ran out of the house. I wore only my nightshift to protect me against the night's air, and I was bareheaded and barefooted as a toddler. Nothing about my nakedness bothered me. I barely noticed. All that I knew was that I had to get to Oma's.

Only adulthood will now allow me to recall that night for what it was. I was brave to run out into the night to save my moeder, but my cowardice drove me just as hard. I was afraid by what I had seen. The blood and the severity of her face had pushed me out of that house just as much as my need to save her. I was afraid of her and afraid to lose her all at the same time.

Little pebbles stuck in my bare feet as I ran through the neighborhoods. I pulled them out in between strides when they became unbearable. Sweat ran down my face and collected under my hair along my neck while I panted through the strides. Tightness gripped my chest the longer I ran. I tried to close my eyes to help me concentrate on breathing, but whenever I did, all I could see behind those eyelids were the images of my moeder lying in a pool of her own blood. She reached out to me and called my name with blood dripping from her fingers. I kept my eyes open.

Ahead of me was the last turn before my Oma's house. I groaned inside when I saw the green roof of the fishery drying shack. It seemed that as soon as I saw it, the smell overwhelmed me, and I collapsed to the ground. My heavy pants turned into wet heaves as I vomited all of my stomach's contents on the dirt next to me.

I knew that I could not fail, and laying there next to my own vomit was failing. I took a deep breath, held it and got to my feet.

Dirty and dizzy, I started running again. I rounded the corner where the drying house was, and ran further. My lungs screamed for air, but I knew that taking another breath now meant smelling that smell again. That smell would land me on my stomach again, and Moeder might die if that happened.

At last, I could see the front door of Oma's house. That sight meant it was safe to breathe, so I drew several ragged breaths into my lungs. I propelled myself up to her door and prayed that she had left it unlocked. She had, and the door opened easily under my direction. I lunged into the house with my lungs on fire and my body screamed with the exertion of the journey.

"Oma!" I screamed with all of the energy I had left within me.

My throat was hoarse and raspy and the sheer exertion of screaming that one word forced me to my knees. I drew in more air and clutched at my dirty legs. It felt like my lungs were going to explode with every ragged breath I took. The next words came out in a whisper because it was all I had left to give.

"Please help us."

Chapter Fourteen

Moeder did not die that night. After seeing all of the blood that covered our kitchen floor, I was sure that she would, but she did not. A carriage came for her in the night and carried her away to Leiden. I stayed with my Oma worrying a hole in the carpet from my pacing. We had heard nothing of her condition, and I knew little of this Leiden place. All I knew was that it was where women were taken to have their babies and sometimes die.

"I do not wish to have children," I told my Oma while I sulked over a glass of milk.

"Oh? Why is that?"

"It seems stupid. Women do this and sometimes they die. All of the trouble is to bring another baby into the house that they cannot feed."

Oma sighed and sat in the chair next to me. I felt her warm hand fold over mine.

"There was a lot of blood was there not, Maria?"

I hesitated as the gruesome scene unraveled itself in front of my eyes again. I could almost smell the rusty scent of the air again. I nodded to her and pushed what remained of my milk away.

"Yes child, I am sure that to you that seemed terrible and unnatural. Believe it or not, that is what women are meant to bear."

"The church men say that it is our punishment for Eve's original sin."

"Yes, I've heard that as well."

I looked at her incredulously. My Oma was no heretic, but her words sounded unconvinced.

"Do you not believe that Oma?"

"Not entirely."

I was shocked. We were not the most devout family, but these were words that just were not spoken out loud.

"Do not look at me like that, Maria. I thought I could speak frankly to you now. You have seen enough, and you are old enough to know truths, are you not?"

I hesitated. I was not sure how to respond.

"If you wish for me to treat as I would a child, I will."

"No. I do not wish that. But Oma, do you not believe in God?"

"Of course, I believe in God. I just do not always subscribe to all of the explanations of the stories. They are told to us by men, and what do men know about child birth?"

I thought on that for a while.

"Then why is it that women have the burden of it?"

"Well, I believe that God is very smart. He charged women with the burden of childbirth because he knew we were the only ones who could do it. If men were the only ones who could have babies, we would not have very many babies in the world."

She smiled at me in a conspiratorial fashion, and I smiled back at her. I still guessed that our conversation was heretical, but it felt good to be a confidant. She pushed my milk towards me. I took it and drank it down.

*   *   *

Vincent returned soon afterwards and took me back to our apartment. He was thin and frail, but I could see health returning in his eyes. He and I were both excited to hear that Sien had had a baby boy, and they both were alive and well. The boy had been born July 2, 1882. The prospect of meeting the new family member made Vincent giddy. He paced about the house cleaning everything like a mother bird preparing her nest. You would have thought the boy was his son. I was more nervous than anything else. I had seen how frail babies were in this world. Better to not become attached.

A visit was planned to see Sien and the new baby in Leiden. Vincent was so excited that he went to the cobbler and bought me new shoes to wear for the occasion. They were the most beautiful pair of shoes I had ever owned, and I immediately worried about the expense. However, since Vincent was not drawing while he recovered, he was not purchasing the expensive art supplies as he normally did. Theo had also been sending us more money while Vincent recovered. I decided to keep quiet and accepted the shoes gratefully.

On the day of the visit, we arrived at Leiden early and dressed as though we were meeting a foreign dignitary. He wore his newly pressed pants and the finest shirt and jacket he owned. I had mended the one hole the jacket had under the arm the night before. His clothes bagged on his thinner frame, but he beamed as though he were dressed like a wealthy merchant. I wore my finest light green dress and the bonnet that I reserved for church. It had only one stain, but it was underneath the tie and not visible. Of course, on my feet were my spectacular new shoes.

A buxom woman with a kind face showed us to Sien's room. She wore white, and I wondered how she laundered her uniform to be so white and well pressed. In fact, everyone in the hospital wore perfectly laundered uniforms. Even the sheets on the patient's beds looked crisp and clean. The entire hospital smelled clean and like sharp cleaning solutions. I suddenly felt dirty and underdressed. My hands unconsciously ran down my dress to try to smooth a wrinkle that wouldn't lay.

I was not sure what to expect when we saw Sien. The last I had seen her, she was pale and covered in blood. I suppose that I was prepared to see her in a bed, barely able to sit up. I pictured her hair to be brittle and caked with sweat. Her eyes would be red rimmed and unfocused. My idea of what I was about to see was not far off from how Vincent had looked when we visited him. I braced myself.

When we entered the room, I saw that the bed was empty and the sheets were immaculately pressed and tucked into the mattress. I looked around the room and found Sien in a chair by the window, gazing out into the garden beyond. She held a white bundle in her arms. When she turned to see us, her face brightened as though someone lit a fire in her cheeks.

I was amazed. Her pallor was rosy, and she seemed to glow from within. I had been certain that after the incident in the kitchen, she would have been near death, but she looked better than I had seen her in years. A sudden thought entered my head. Vincent should paint her as she was right then. If he did that, then his painting might actually be beautiful.

"Maria, see how lovely your moeder is today? She is amazing. Go to her," whispered Vincent in my ear.

I did, barely able to believe this was my moeder.

"Maria, come here and meet your brother," said Sien.

At the sound of her voice, the little bundle stirred and whimpered. I moved closer to her and peeked at the moving mass in her arms. A tiny, pink face was in among the blankets, as wrinkled and raw as a woman getting out of a scalding bath. His eyes were shut and his tiny mouth puckered and suckled the air as though looking for a breast in his sleep. He was perfect, and I loved him instantly. Warmth swelled in my chest as I watched him squirm.

"Would you like to hold him?"

I did not have words, they had suddenly left me. Vincent moved silently to my left side, and I could feel his warm presence. He laid a gentle hand on my back, and I was jolted out of my trance.

"Yes, please."

Much shuffling occurred before the tiny baby was placed into my arms. He was barely heavier than a kitten. I could feel his little legs shift in the blanket, and his hand went to his face while he yawned. He made not a sound as he opened his eyes and stared up into mine. We stayed there in that miracle of a moment for a while, his purple blue eyes looking up into my dark brown ones. I smiled down at him and understood instantly why women had babies. No longer did I think this was an idiot's folly. This child was everything, and everything revolved around him.

When I looked back up, I caught Sien looking at my new shoes. I froze, realizing what the expense must look like to her. Such a luxury was ridiculous with a new baby here, and all at once, I looked frivolous to myself. I wanted to tell her that we would return them the moment we got back home, but when she looked back up at me, she smiled in a grand way.

"Those are lovely, Maria. I have been meaning to buy you a decent pair all year."

Relief washed over me, and all of my apologies dissipated in the wind. Instead, I asked a far more important question.

"What is his name?"

"Willem Vincent Hoornik."

"Willem," I whispered to the baby. "Your name is Willem. You are my Willem, and I will never let you go."

Chapter Fifteen

After seeing Willem, I inherited Vincent's need to nest; and thus, the apartment was cleaned with the meticulous enthusiasm only reserved for the insane. We washed our linens over and over again, never seeming to get them clean enough, and the floors were scrubbed so rigorously that the grooves of the wood smoothed and no longer caught our clothing as we walked past.

Theo had sent Vincent more money after hearing about the baby's birth, and he promised to send still more for us in the future. Most of it went to the repairs and preparations for Sien and Willem's return. Vincent bought a used basinet from the wet nurse three streets from us. It was in good condition and would be perfect. We also found a charwoman who was selling her rich family's old baby blankets. They were no longer able to have children due to an illness, and the blankets were a painful reminder to them. The wife had given them to her, but she was too old to have children. She sold them to us at a very cheap price.

It was not until the landlord visited us one day in response to our request for new paper for the walls that we stopped our work. He had brought us the interesting news that the apartment next door was vacant. Not only that, but he was currently repapering the walls in it, and he would not charge us the extra fee for the new paper if we wanted to move in right away. The apartment was larger, but the rent was more expensive. I thought to turn the man down immediately, but Vincent said that we would consider it.

After the landlord left, I looked at Vincent with an air of skepticism.

"What is it, Little Cat?"

"Are you really thinking about moving into the apartment next door?"

"Yes. Why would we not?"

"It is more expensive."

"Yes, it is, but Theo is sending me more money."

I was silent.

"Do not look at me in that way."

"In what way?"

"In that way that is so very like your moeder. I do not plan to depend on my family long, Little Cat. I have already begun to earn commissions, and soon, I hope to support us with my drawings."

I looked skeptical again.

"It will happen, and we will be a family. A growing family needs more room like a flower needs room to blossom."

I thought to myself that a flower also needs food to grow, but I did not dare say it. Vincent was in such good spirits, and I did not want to start a fight with him.

"You would have your own room in the new apartment."

He said this in the manner adults do when trying to tempt small children with a treat. My first reaction was to be insulted, especially since I was making great strides to be less childlike. However, I had to admit that the idea of my own room was tempting. I remained stoic.

"I already have my own room."

"You have a crawl space. It is supposed to be used as an extra pantry. That is no place for a girl. Besides, you will outgrow it in a year."

He was right of course. The little room I had was already small for me. If I stretched out completely, my feet touched the wall. With a little more height I would have to curl my feet in to sleep there comfortably.

"I see your head working, Little Cat. You know that I am right. Your moeder and I would have a bigger room, and there would be a space off of my studio for Willem's basinet. I saw the place when I visited our neighbors before they moved away. There is an alcove in a room perfect for a studio. We could curtain it with some fabric and make it a nursery. Would that not be a nicer nest for Sien and Willem to come home to? Think of the joy on her face."

A thought entered my mind when he mentioned the studio.

"The studio, it is bigger?"

"Oh yes, much bigger."

"And the light is better?"

He looked at me quizzically, wary of my sudden interest.

"Yes, from what I remember. When I visited the previous tenants before, there was a large window that allowed for far more light than the one I have now."

"Good. I think we should move then."

"You do? What made you change your mind so suddenly?"

I took a deep breath and let it out.

"If you are going to get more commissions to support us, you will need a better space."

"Oh?"

"Yes, you need the practice."

Chapter Sixteen

We moved into the new apartment before Sien came home from Leiden. Vincent and I did it together. I carried each delicate drawing and book as though they were precious tokens made of porcelain. They might be what would buy us bread in the future, so I made sure that they were just as immaculate when I delivered them as they were when I collected them.

Oma came over to the new home to help to rearrange furniture. We fretted over the basinet endlessly until it looked perfect. We stocked the pantry full of food, and I was pleased to put food in the pantry rather than bedding. My room looked enormous to me, so much so that I had a difficult time sleeping in a space so open and empty. Oma found some extra cushions she had and fashioned them around my bed like a small cave. I could crawl in and out at my leisure, and the cave made me feel safe and secure. I soon was able to sleep well again.

Sien and Willem came home to a beautifully clean and spacious apartment. I worried that Moeder would see the new place and be unhappy knowing the expense. Like the new shoes, I thought she surely would disapprove of the costliness of our new life. However, she seemed oblivious to the extravagance and only beamed with pride and happiness. She lifted little Willem up to show him his new home.

"Look, Willem! Look around you at what your father and sister have done for us."

I tensed at the mention of Vincent as Willem's father. We all knew better, so why did she say that? I opened my mouth to contradict Moeder when Oma put her hand on my shoulder. I looked up into her eyes that were looking down at me. She was giving me a look of warning. When I almost said something again, she squeezed my shoulder and shook her head slowly.

"Let her pretend," whispered Oma. "Look how happy it makes them."

I looked at the spectacle in front of me. Sien was glowing with pride as she lifted Willem in the air and made a great show of handing him over to Vincent, who seemed completely delighted with his new title of father. Vincent always spoke about marrying Sien someday when he began making his own money with his artwork. They both laughed and smiled as I had not seen in a long time.

I nodded and said nothing.

*   *   *

Life became lovely. Moeder stopped drinking and her milk flowed freely to little Willem's mouth. We ate as we liked, within reason. Moeder would not dare to overspend on luxuries, but we never lacked good bread, cheese, or the occasional sausage. She attained more seamstress work, and I had gotten good enough with buttons and small patches to help her. The work went faster, which meant we were paid sooner.

Vincent received even more money from Theo, and his parents sent an extra sum to help him with his recovery. I watched him gain some of his weight back. His color also improved by incredible degrees. He even began to draw again, but this time, he included the entire family. Even with part of our money going back to paying for art supplies, we were still not to point of black bread and water like we had been.

Of course, most of our cheer could be attributed to little Willem. The babe was a charming sort and so well behaved. He rarely cried or whimpered, except during the times when babies normally do. We would hear from him when he was hungry or wet, but rarely any other time. He was happy and smiled a great deal. It was difficult to be melancholy when you looked into his chubby face so full of blissful ignorance. He had no care or thought about the harshness of life and knew only the warm embrace of family. I envied him and spoiled him.

It was one evening when we all rested in Vincent's studio that he first mentioned painting. He was sketching little Willem trying to raise himself on his hands and knees, Moeder was sewing in her chair, and I was sitting on the floor next to Vincent watching him draw.

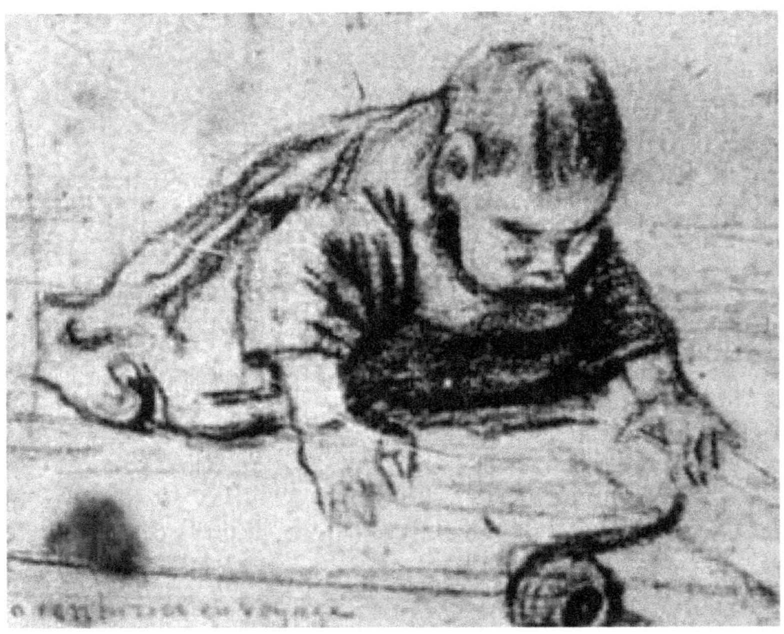

"I am so happy these days. It would be a shame not to capture these moments better. Perhaps I should pick up painting again."

"Again? Did you paint before?"

"Yes, Little Cat. I painted a little, but they were no good. My family suggested that I learn to draw first since that is how the masters did it. They said I should master drawing, and then my paintings would be better."

I said nothing, but he could read my silence.

"I take it you think I need more practice at drawing?"

I shrugged.

"You are better."

"Maria!" exclaimed Sien from her chair.

I shrunk inside myself, and Vincent laughed.

"Sien, it is all right. I need an honest critic. Maria is the best I know. All the honesty of a critic but none of the cruelty."

"She still should not speak to you like that."

Moeder glowered at me, and I shrunk inside myself further. I detested it when Moeder yelled at me, especially when it was for no good reason. Just then, Willem whimpered and cried at all of the sudden noise. Exasperated, Sien got up from her chair and collected the baby in her arms.

"See what you two have done now?" She stormed off to feed the crying child in the other room. I looked down at the drawing Vincent had been working on. It really was better. That part was true. I supposed that it was difficult to draw something terrible with such a delightful little fellow as a model.

"Do not fret, Little Cat," whispered Vincent as though we were conspirators in a story. "I expect you to be just as honest about my paintings as you are about my drawings."

I smiled because I knew I would.

Chapter Seventeen

For a while, we were a happy family, but it all changed on the day that Tersteeg darkened our door. He was a man not unlike an uncle to Vincent. Until that point I had heard Vincent utter only the most glowing remarks about the man's kindness and encouragement. Tersteeg had shown Vincent immense kindness when he needed it the most, and without it, Vincent might have not dared to try his hand at art. Vincent kept a small paint box that Tersteeg had given him and a collection of model books by someone named Charles Bargue. They were great treasures to him. He always showed it to me as though I should know who Charles Bargue was, but I did not.

After the conversations with Vincent, I had pictured a man who practically glowed with virtue. I believed that he had to be one of the kindest souls in The Hague, and I asked multiple times when we might meet him. The virtuous demon arrived on our doorstep unannounced one Thursday afternoon.

"Vincent!"

The word had come from our front doorstep, but it was barked more than spoken. We looked at each other quizzically before we stood from our places and followed Vincent to the door. He opened the door to greet a slight man dressed in a fashionable suit. His hair was cut short and he had a beard that tapered dramatically to a point. His mustache was trimmed to fit and blend into his cone of a beard perfectly. He had eyes that seemed too big for his face. They were full of anger.

"Tersteeg! What a pleasant surprise. I am so glad that you have come for a visit. Please enter, dear friend. May I offer you some water or coffee?"

"No," he grumbled as he marched inside.

Moeder and I watched from the studio entranceway without words. I could not help but think that I had misheard Vincent. Surely this could not be the benevolent Tersteeg I had heard him speak of over and over again.

"Well then, what do I owe the honor of your visit? I wish you had told me. We could have arranged for some supper."

Vincent's tone was cheerful despite Tersteeg's rough entrance and judging eyes. Tersteeg waved him away as his eyes darted around the room. He looked around the apartment as though he were looking for something in particular. I wondered what he was trying to find.

"That will not be necessary. I am here because I have been in correspondence with your brother, Theo. After what he told me, I had to come see this for myself."

His voice was raised and the sharpness of it woke Willem. He had been sleeping peacefully in his studio basinet, but now, he wailed with fright. The very air in the apartment went tense with the sound of his cries.

"That is what I thought."

Tersteeg turned and stormed toward the studio with a rage that terrified me. All I could think of was to run to the baby, so I did just that. I raced to the basinet ahead of the man and stood my ground in front of it. I defiantly glared up at Tersteeg with all of the will I could muster. Whatever Tersteeg's intentions, he would have to go through me to get to Willem. My glare did nothing. He just looked past me to the child I protected as though I were not there.

"What is this meaning of this child? How could you think of living with this woman and children in the bargain? Is it not just as ridiculous as driving my own four-in-hand through the city for everyone to see? Have you gone mad? This is certainly a thing that came from an unsound mind and temperament."

"Please, sir. You do not understand. I have not lost my mind. We are happy here as a family."

"A family? Pray tell me that this creature is not of your blood."

"No, he is not mine in blood, but I love him as though he were."

"Madness! All of this is madness. I knew you were a man plagued by an unsound mind at times, but Vincent, this is pure lunacy."

Sien had moved aside for the intrusion, and she began to sob into her hands. Shock was written all over her face. I was exasperated with the pair of them. Vincent cowered to Tersteeg, and Moeder wept like a frightened child. Neither of them had the courage to move. I wanted to stand up for our family, but how could I battle the demon alone? He still acted as though Sien and I were not in the same room as he. We breathed the same air, yet we did not warrant our own existence.

"I will tell your parents of this blasphemy. They will hear of this child, and they will know where all of their money is going."

"I have kept nothing from them. I recently sent a letter inviting them to come here for a visit at my expense. I would love for them to see how happy we are."

"Your expense? You truly have lost your mind. It would not be at *your* expense at all. It would be at Theo's expense and your parents' expense. They would be paying for a trip to visit a whore and her bastards."

I had the sudden urge to kick the man, but I repressed it. Vincent looked appalled, and Sien sobbed louder.

"I am making money for myself more and more these days, Tersteeg. Look here," said Vincent as he pointed to his drawings that lined the wall. "See how I am improving? Soon, I will be commissioned to make more works."

Tersteeg glanced over the drawings for an instant before he waved his hand dismissing them.

"These are old. I have seen these."

"But see, some of them are new. I have shown them to no one."

Vincent tried in vain to get Tersteeg to look over them and concede that there were fresh drawings, but the man was unmovable.

"C.M. was a fool to buy even the first ones from you. I would not count on anymore charity from the man if I were you. I will speak to him, and you will not receive another coin for your art in this city."

"But if you just look Tersteeg, you will see that I am improving."

Tersteeg scoffed and rolled his eyes back in the directly of Willem and me.

"This is lunacy, Vincent."

"This is my family, sir."

Vincent's brow furrowed, and he stood face to face with the demon himself. Neither man was large in stature, and I wondered who would win if this escalated into a fight. In any case, I was ready to kick the demon if the need arose.

"I will tell your parents, and this family you hold so dear will end."

At that, Tersteeg turned and left our home in the same way he had entered. He had been a storm cloud of anger that rained over our happy life, and when he left, we were never the same. It was as if a piece him stayed in the very walls in order to haunt our lives.

Tersteeg. Tersteeg.

No longer did that name bring about images of a benevolent uncle with kind eyes and a dear heart. Instead, I cursed that named until the end of my days.

Chapter Eighteen

The very air in our apartment changed after that. Sien blamed Vincent for not standing up for us like the family we were. I had to admit, I did too to an extent. His performance during Tersteeg's visit had seemed like the worst kind of cowardice. His argument was that he was too stunned by the man's sudden anger to know how to react. I understood that too. Far be it for me to pass judgment on anyone's behavior when my own moeder stood aside and watched it in tears. I was disappointed in them both, and secretly, I wished that I had kicked the man. Consequences be damned.

Our joy had been replaced with an unease that was far worse than sorrow, far worse than most emotions. Sien began to sneak bottles home again. She never thought we knew, but how could I not see her? She hid them at the bottom of her market baskets and piled food on top of them in an effort to conceal her crimes. I first saw it one afternoon when we had not had as much money to buy food. With fewer objects to hide the bottle, I watched her quickly slide the atrocity under Baby Willem's swaddling blankets. The few potatoes and bread she had would no longer hide it well enough.

Vincent did not see this. It was not that Sien was clever in her deceit; it was just that he ceased to notice happenings outside of his studio. The man had become obsessed with proving Tersteeg wrong. He spent hours upon hours shut away in his studio, painting and drawing. He had regained his zeal for art, but had lost his touch with the family. I hated when he was this way. Vincent barely spoke to us and often took his meals in his studio. I tried on several occasions to peek over his shoulder and offer my advice, but he had no patience for intruders and ordered me away.

Vincent began ordering more art supplies again, and this time they were mainly painting supplies. I did not know the exact difference, only that painting supplies were quite a bit more expensive. Paints required colors, and colors required Vincent paying some expensive man who sold him raw pigments. He would mix the pigments with oils that smelled strong to make his paints. After a while, the stronger our apartment smelled of oil, the more our monthly food rations dwindled to a depressing level.

One day, he offered to take Sien and me into the country for a day trip into the woods. So pleased were we that we hummed pleasant songs while we packed a lunch and dressed in fine attire. Moeder wore a white dress she had made while in Leiden with a new summer hat that had a stark red ribbon tied across it. Oma had made the hat for her as a homecoming gift. I wore a black short dress my Oma had made for me with a white frilled hat. My hat I had made myself, and I was proud of the way it fit. It had been my finest finished hat project, and I had made it with only a little help from Oma. We looked nice, and we felt like regal women on an outing to the countryside.

The day was perfect for a trip. I had high hopes that the outing would remedy most of the sour emotions that seemed to fly around our heads. It was the very later part of autumn, and the sky was clean and crisp with the last bits of warm air swirling around us. I could not remember the last time I had seen the sky so blue, and the leaves of the swaying trees were just beginning to change color. None had fallen to the ground yet, but we could all tell that the threat of it was present.

We arrived at the picnicking area near the woods, and all seemed to be in high spirits. Sien was sober and happy as she laid out a blanket and prepared our lunch. Willem cooed and giggled from his basket as the rays of sunshine danced across his tiny feet. Even Vincent scowled less as he setup his easel and paints near the blanket.

After lunch, we found out that Vincent's real reason for bringing us to the country was to paint more landscapes. Apparently, C.M. had told him that his portfolio was lacking in landscapes, so Vincent intended to remedy that in the country with us. Sien looked a little sad at the revelation that Vincent had not intended the outing to be for family fun, but I was not sad at all. If Vincent was to become a great artist who could support us on his own, he would need to do what C.M. said.

I offered to model in the woods with an enthusiasm that infected Sien immediately. We would enjoy this outing together no matter what, and we would help Vincent with his craft. I had been consumed with the same overwhelming need that Vincent had to prove Tersteeg wrong. I thought again about how I should have kicked him.

Vincent seemed to be unimpressed by our enthusiasm to help his cause, but he did concede that having a model in the painting would be beneficial. We moved our party into the woods, and Vincent set up there to paint us among the enormous trees. Willem stayed with me while Moeder posed, and she took care of him while I posed. While it was cooler in the shade of the trees, I found that standing still on the uneven earth was more difficult that sitting still on the flat floor of the studio. Sweat collected under my hair and wetted the scarf of my dress. The exertion caused sweat to roll slowly down my legs and collect in my shoes. It was entirely uncomfortable, but I was determined not to move.

When we were done, I walked over to Vincent to see the two canvases that he had been working on. I peered past him as he packed away all of his paints and brushes. What I saw shocked me. After all of that time and energy, Moeder and I were but blobs of color. You could not even tell that it was us.

"What are those?"

Vincent turned to me.

"What do you mean?"

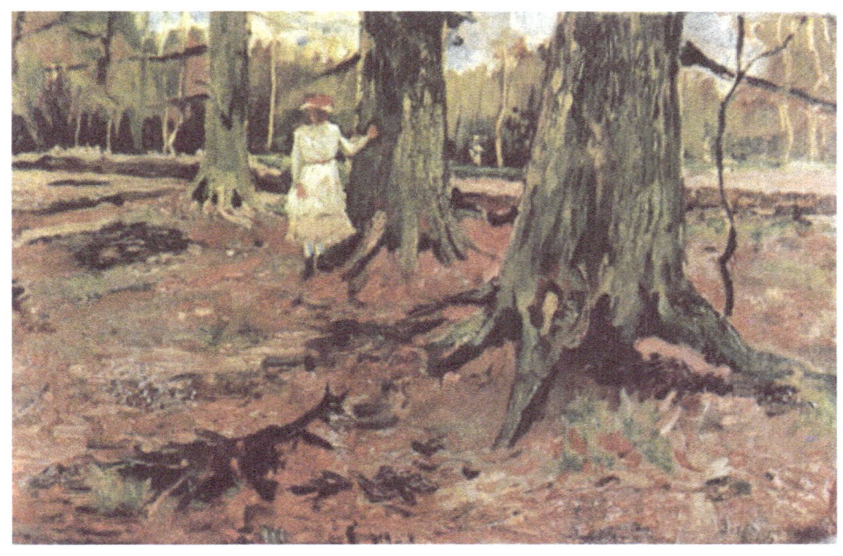

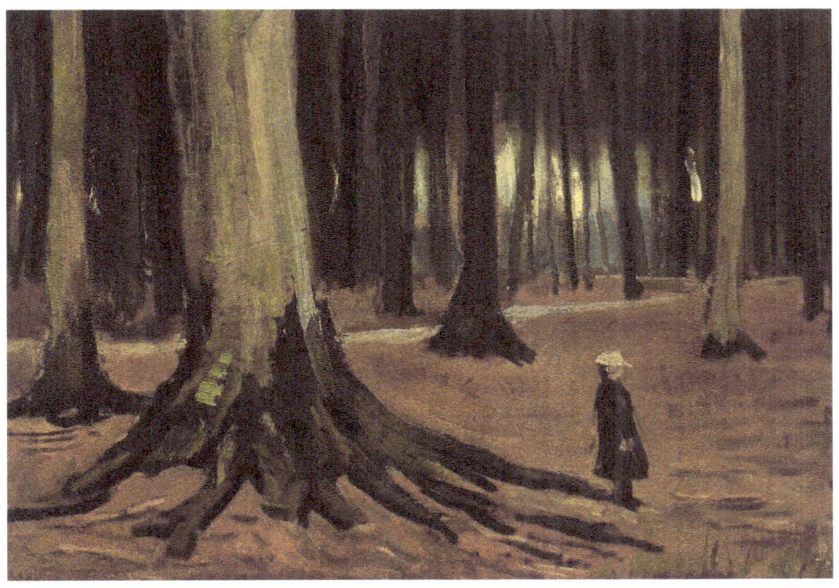

"Are those the paintings of me and Moeder?"

"Yes. Do you not like them? Look at how I rendered the trees. I think it is a good show of light and will make an excellent addition to my portfolio."

"I do not like them."

"Why?"

"Because the women in the painting do not look like us. We are only blobs of paint. In your drawings, Moeder looks like her, and I look like me."

"These painting are not about you. They are about the trees and the light of the day. You and Sien are like adding flowers, an afterthought."

The insult stung as though he had slapped my face.

"We are no afterthought!"

I was enraged. We had sacrificed our afternoon and stood still, sweating in our finer clothes, to be daubs of paint among his beautiful trees. We were an afterthought to him, and he did not seem to mind. What had happened to our family?

"Maria, do not shout."

I gasped at the sound of my name. Vincent had not called me Maria in months. I had been Little Cat to him, and the fact that he reverted to my actual name hurt in a way I could not explain.

"Little Cat."

"What?"

I stormed away from him exasperated beyond belief.

"My name is Little Cat!" I shouted back at him over my shoulder.

I wanted to shout at him that I hated his paintings, but he had not asked my opinion. That fact alone wounded my pride like an arrow through a buck's leg. My indignity knew no target, and I fell to weeping behind a tree where no one could see me. It was a harsh thing to learn the pain of suddenly not mattering to someone you love. To be an ally and trusted friend one day and an anonymous paint daub the next was a new kind of pain for me. I vowed to not speak to Vincent for seven days as punishment for this insult. I wondered if he would notice.

Chapter Nineteen

It turned out that Vincent did finally notice me and my vow of silence, but it took three days of ignoring him. He dismissed my insults as childish and completely beneath the way I normally conducted myself. He never seemed to want to admit that he had been wrong or mean in any fashion. Apologies were rarely a factor in his world.

His mood swings were something I learned to deal with and tried in vain to predict. One minute, he was happy and ready to talk with me. The same day might also find him melancholy and held up in the darkness of his studio with the curtain drawn. I knew not to disturb him when he was truly focused on his artwork. His eyes seemed to narrow to points of concentration, and this was the time when he cared for no one. Knowing what mood he would be in became a fine art in itself. I quickly became a master of that art. Stomping around and yelling did nothing to help matters. Instead, I danced the dance of invisibility when he brooded this way. It was the only way to keep my friend and refrain from vowing a punishment of silence on a regular basis.

The beginning of autumn marked two special events for me. One event was my eighth birthday, and I was quite happy to be turning such a prestigious age. At least, at the time, I thought it was prestigious. Any age older than seven sounded wonderful, and on September twenty-seventh, I would turn eight years old.

The second event arrived the day before my birthday. An old man wearing a worn seamen's uniform walked through our door and greeted Vincent as though they were friends. I sat at our kitchen table completely mesmerized by the cut of his hair. He wore a top hat, and under the hat, his hair was fashioned into salt and pepper waves. However, he had grown his facial hair such that blossomed from his ear and billowed down the side of his face. He had cut off its progression at the chin at a sharp angle. The truly fascinating part was that while the hair on his head was salt and pepper, the hair on his face was stark white. It was a truly odd sight.

The old man tipped his hat to me as he and Vincent walked past the table and into the studio. I leaped up from the table, kicked off my shoes, and walked as quietly as I could to the studio door. It was opened a crack, so I peered in at the two men.

"Where would you like me?" asked the old man.

His voice sounded smooth and calming.

"Well, what is comfortable for you, Mr. Zuijderland?"

"Well, I prefer to sit if I can. At seventy-two, I am not quite the spry lad I once was."

He chuckled at his own joke, and Vincent laughed politely.

"Sitting would be fine, sir. I will just move this chair by the window here. This position makes for some nice lighting."

The old man moved and took his place in the chair by the window. I noticed that he had some kind of medal on his lapel and a number sewn onto sleeve. My curiosity was becoming overwhelmed. I thought that surely this man could not be a real man. There were far too many strange and unanswered bits to him to be real.

"How is this?"

Vincent positioned himself around the old man, and settled in to draw.

"That is perfect, Mr. Zuijderland. Just hold that pose as still as you can."

"I will do my best, but is the mouse outside the door going to join us too?"

I froze where I stood and went cold all over. I had been discovered. Vincent only chuckled with good humor.

"Ah, but that is no mouse, sir."

He stood up, walked over to the studio door, and flung it open. I had been found out. There was no place to run and hide. Vincent had exposed me. I stared at the two men who were smiling down at me.

"This our Little Cat."

"Ah, a Little Cat. I always did like cats."

I stood in the doorway, unsure what I should do. I thought about apologizing, but these men did not seem cross in any way.

"Well, may the cat join us? She does not look big enough to cause any harm."

"Well, that is up to her. Would you like to join us, Maria?"

I looked up at Vincent, and he winked at me. If he was alright with me being there, then I should be as such. I nodded and stepped into the room. Vincent went back to his position behind the paper. I sat on the floor. I tried not to stare at the old man's facial hair, but it was difficult to look away.

"Maria, is it? It is alright if I speak, Vincent?"

"Yes, just do not move your head. I'll tell you when I am drawing your mouth."

I nodded to him. "Yes, my name is Maria."

"Greetings, Maria, the Little Cat. My name is Adrianus Jacobus Zuijderland, and I am at your service."

I furrowed my brow in puzzlement at him.

"My service, sir? What service is that?"

"Any service that you might need. I could never refuse a lady."

"Is that why you wear that uniform, Mr. Zuijderland? Were you in service to someone?"

"Oh, not just someone. I was in the service of our great country. I fought in the Ten Days Campaign of Holland against the terrible Belgians. I was so brave they gave me the Metal Cross for my valor. See it there?"

I looked at the medal on his label and nodded. It was thoroughly impressive. Never had I met a war hero before. I smiled at him.

"And those numbers on your sleeve, are they from the war?"

I saw Vincent tense a little, but Mr. Zuijderland only smiled.

"Once you get her talking, she is full of questions," he mused to Vincent before he addressed me. "No, my dear. These numbers are for the almshouse where I reside."

I was taken aback. It was hard to believe that such a valiant man would ever be seen at an old person's almshouse. I had seen the type of people who lived there. They were usually decrepit and some could barely walk.

"The numbers are for the residents, you see. If one of us loses our wits and gets lost, whoever finds us will know where to take us. Plus, the almshouse will know who we are by the number. It is all very organized."

I must have looked worried and confused.

"No worries, Little Cat. I rarely lose my wits. At least, I have not yet today."

He winked at me, but Vincent chided him for moving, so he stopped.

As the conversation continued, I learned that Vincent had walked over to Mr. Zuijderland's almshouse the day before to ask if any of the residents might want to volunteer their services as a model. He could not pay them much, but he would offer a small fee and a mug of coffee. One older woman had slapped his face for his indecency, and the others just ignored him. Mr. Zuijderland was the only one who volunteered. He had said that he wanted to do it more for the idea of getting out of the almshouse and breathing some fresh air than anything else. Apparently, old people smelled to him, and he was sick of breathing them into his lungs.

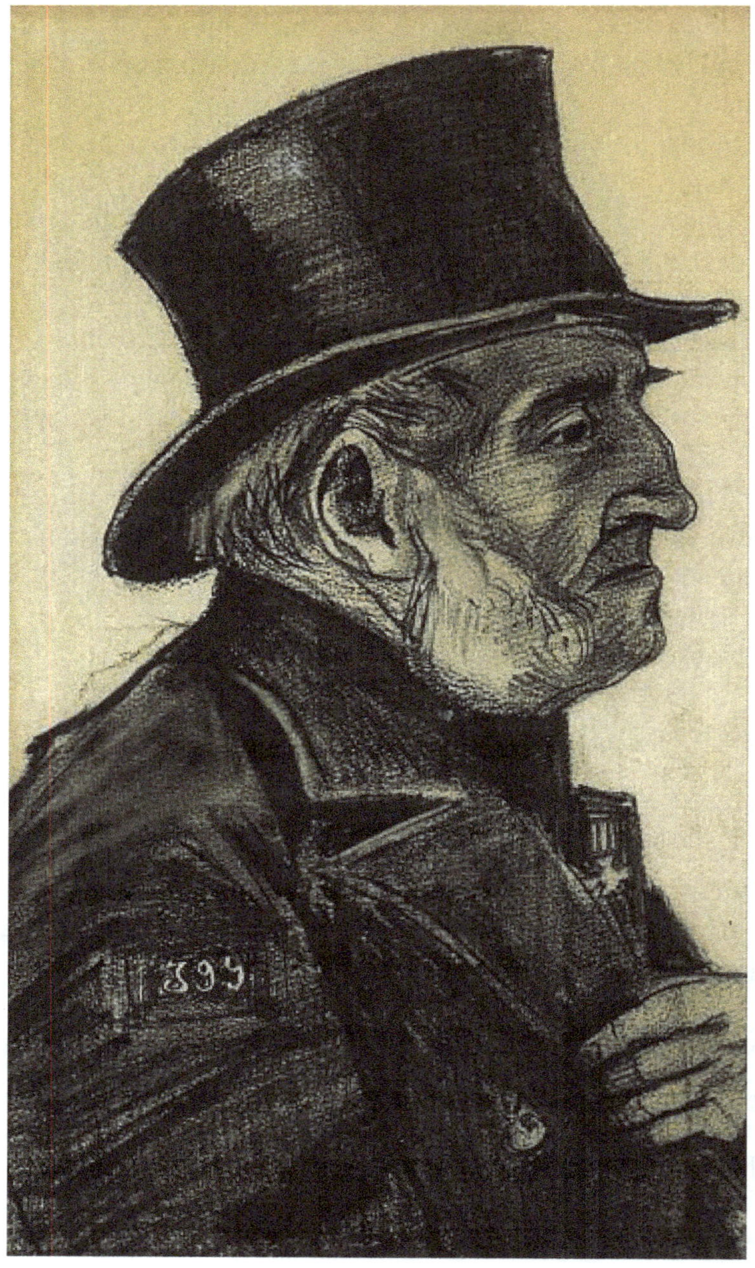

When Vincent finished the drawing, he left us alone in the room to look it over. It did look like Mr. Zuijderland. Vincent even got the strange facial hair to look proper. I wanted to gaze longer at the drawing, but Vincent had left that little blue book out on the table. My eyes kept straying to it like they always did. I sometimes thought that if I could concentrate hard enough, I could understand the letters on the cover. Of course, that never worked. It remained gibberish to me.

"Something caught your interest?" asked Mr. Zuijderland when he caught me looking away.

I stuttered a bit before pointing out the blue book on the table. The old man reached for it and smiled as he gazed upon the cover.

"Ah, I love this one. *Les Miserables* by Victor Hugo. Why are you so intent on this one?"

He too could read, and he had read the blue book that haunted my dreams. I was not sure what to say, so I said nothing.

"Can you read this book?"

I looked around us for Vincent. He was still in the kitchen making Mr. Zuijderland his coffee. I shook my head slowly.

"Would you like to learn how to read this book?"

My eyes widened with shock. I could barely believe what he had said to me.

"I can teach you to read this if you would like."

He smiled so warmly at me, and I felt my chest fill with happiness. If Mr. Zuijderland taught me to read, I would know what Vincent knew. I would be able to read and understand his artists. The little blue book would no longer be the great mystery of my life. He would never learn the truth and think me stupid. Then, a sudden realization hit me in the stomach. My eyes dropped and I exhaled all of the happy emotions out of my lungs.

"Mr. Zuijderland, I would love it if you taught me to read, but I have no way to pay you."

I stared down at my bare feet.

"Maria, you do not have to pay me."

"No?"

"No. I heard from Vincent that your birthday is tomorrow."

"Yes, it is!"

"Consider this my birthday gift to you. I can see that you and I will be great friends, and friends give each other gifts on their birthdays. Besides, you have given me another excuse to enjoy some fresh air instead of breathing nothing but old people's air."

He smiled and winked at me, and we whispered like conspirators.

"You must not tell Vincent."

He nodded without question.

"It is a matter between you and me. I will not speak a word of it to anyone."

The next day, there was a dinner for our family. Oma came to the house, and everyone celebrated my birthday. There was meat and drinking, and, for that evening, everyone seemed happy again. I received several wonderful gifts for which I was very grateful, but none of them could compare to Mr. Zuijderland's secret gift. It was the best gift anyone had ever given me, and I could tell no one about it.

Chapter Twenty

Even though the nasty Tersteeg never darkened our door again, we still felt the icy chill of his presence. After he left, the envelopes from Vincent's family began to dwindle. I soon learned to recognize the sender by the color of the envelope they sent. The yellow ones, which were from Theo, seemed to arrive regularly. The white ones were from Vincent's parents, and they came more sporadically.

After Tersteeg's threats to reveal the true nature of our family to Vincent's father, the white envelopes came to our door less and less. We all began to take a page from Vincent's obsession and waited impatiently for the post every day. The three of us shared the same defeat every time we sifted through the letters to find none of the white envelopes yet again. Moeder often asked Vincent about it, but he would dress his face in a smile and tell her not to worry.

"Tersteeg has spun lies about us to my parents, and I am currently writing a letter that will dispel all of those rumors. Everything will be well."

Talk like that placated her for a short time, but when Vincent gave her half the money he normally handed her for the weekly market trip, Sien asked him again.

"They are stubborn and listening to falsities. Tersteeg has been a loyal friend to them, and my history as a son has not always been a virtuous one. I have written several letters to my brother, Theo. He will help me convince them of the truth. He is a true brother and friend."

It was not long before the white envelopes all but ceased, and the yellow ones from Theo began to dwindle. Food was beginning to get harder to acquire, and the cold of winter was threatening our city. Vincent championed his brother still.

"He is worried about taking sides in the matter. They are his family as well. I am telling you that my family will see the light. I have written them all explaining how happy we are here. I tell them that your children are my children. We have finally found a happy home, and we want to rejoice in it with them. I assure them that we budget our expenses very carefully and buy nothing extravagant. If we could get them to visit us, they would see it for themselves."

The time came when Vincent knew the postman's schedule by memory. I often found him waiting by the front door eagerly awaiting a letter from anyone. The yellow envelopes from Theo still came, but they were fewer. Plus, they held less and less money. Apparently, the message was clear. His family loved him but not his whore.

One day, Sien was complaining about how little money she had to buy our food. Vincent had his head in his hands, trying to block out the sound of her voice. He was pacing back and forth. The look on his face was one that normally told me to become invisible.

"What do you want me to do?" he asked with anger in his throat.

"I want you to get us more money," retorted Sien.

"I cannot. I have disgraced myself to the point of writing my family to tell them that we are cold and hungry. I wrote a letter begging like a common street urchin. What more do you want?"

"Well, you could start by not bringing up lithography again," she spat.

He stood suddenly and pointed a dirtied finger at her.

"You have no right to limit my artistic growth."

"You can grow with charcoal. It is cheaper."

"I must get better, Sien. If I do not, we shall be begging for handouts always. If I am to marry you, I must make a living on my own first."

"You would have us with a studio full of lithography supplies and a pantry full of cobwebs?"

"I would have us live an honest life where we can be happy. I have created successful lithographs in the past. The time has come to visit that again."

To my great relief, there came a knock on the door to interrupt them. It was the postman with a package for Vincent Van Gogh. The mood in the kitchen lightened as we bid farewell to the deliverer of what we hoped was good news.

Vincent placed the package on the kitchen table. I stared at it in wonder. It was a rather large package, and I could taste the curiosity on my tongue. We all ripped into it like savages. I had lovely thoughts about what might be inside. It could be food or perhaps there was money at the bottom of all the paper we ripped from inside the box. I even dared to dream that there might be both.

The contents included a man's winter coat, a woman's winter coat, a small winter coat, and a blanket. Vincent also pulled forth a letter in a white envelope with tears in his eyes. He opened and read it right there in front of us. Whatever the letter read, he was truly touched. You could see it scribbled across his face.

"I knew it. I knew that my parents would see my side of all of this. This is a wonderful sign that they are not as angry as they seemed."

He hugged the coats as though they were his parents themselves.

"Did they send any money?" asked Sien.

"No, but this is better than money. These two coats could only be for you two, and the blanket is for Little Willem. They are not forsaking us. These are gifts you would send to a family. Oh, this is a joyful day!"

Sien and I looked at one another and thought the same thing. They had sent this because Vincent had told them that we were cold and hungry. They could have sent money or food, but they sent what would keep our blood off of their hands. We felt far from accepted, and when Vincent's back was turned, we rummaged through the paper and the box to see if any money had been missed.

Chapter Twenty One

The weeks rolled by us, and Mr. Zuijderland came to pose for Vincent more and more. The old man was a breath of fresh air to our home. I never tired of hearing him talk or of our lessons. He kept his word to me that he would not tell Vincent that he was teaching me to read. I never knew what he told Vincent. All I knew was that after he was finished modeling, he and I would retire to the studio and practice my letters by ourselves. No one ever disturbed us.

It was a hard idea to understand at first. The letters all made certain sounds, but when you put them together, they made whole words that meant something else. When you read a line of words together, they made a sentence. It was all very confusing.

Slowly, but surely, the words made more sense, and the sentences followed suit. I began to put together small sentences of my own. Of course, my goal was the little blue book. I wanted to read that book above all others. It held a certain mystic allure for me that no other book had. For that reason, Mr. Zuijderland always ended our lesson with a short reading from that book. I think he could tell that the act, no matter how small, quelled a desire inside me that I could not explain. He knew it would keep me going even when I got frustrated.

That particular day, I had read halfway through the page all by myself. Normally, Mr. Zuijderland would point out certain words or phrases for me to read in the book, but this time, I was able to put a lot of the sentences together. I linked together phrases and words that I had learned before, and he looked very proud of me.

"He was good-looking…although of small…um."

"It is a difficult one, but you know it, Maria. Think about the letters that make up the word."

"Stat…Stature."

"Very good. Continue, please."

"He was good-looking although of small stature, elegant, graceful and enter…entertaining; his early life was wholly dev…devoted to worldly matters and affairs of gall…antry…gallantry."

"Maria, that is excellent. Truly remarkable."

"Thank you, Mr. Zuijderland."

He knew that I did not know what all of the words meant, but I was reading them out loud quite a bit better.

"I am not just saying that either. I am very impressed. I taught a dozen seamen these same lessons, grown lads too, and not a one progressed as well as you."

"But I do not understand everything yet. When will all of this make sense to me? How long will it take for me to read a whole book?"

"Time is what you need. It will all make sense in time, I assure you. No one understands something this complicated immediately. You are moving faster than most adults I know. Try not to be impatient. Take a moment to celebrate every little accomplishment without dwelling on how far you still have to go. Trust me when I say that you deserve a celebration, Maria. Be happy with your success."

I smiled feeling pleased with myself. Mr. Zuijderland patted me on the back.

A new question formed in my mind. It was a question that I dared not to ask Vincent, and Sien would have no concept of the answer. I was sure of that. Perhaps, Mr. Zuijderland would know. He seemed to know so many things.

"Mr. Zuijderland, do you know what lithography is?"

"Lithography? What makes you ask about that?"

I hesitated, unsure how to word my concerns.

"I overheard Vincent speaking about it to Moeder. Do you know what it is?"

"Yes, I do. Well, I have heard of such things. When you are as old as I am, you get to see all sorts of things. It is a type of art, I think. I believe it is a type of print making."

I shot him a confused look.

"You know, the type of art where you make it once, but you can make many copies of the same thing."

"Oh," I said remembering his Sorrow drawing. "I think I have seen him do that before."

"Why do you ask about lithography?"

I sighed, but much of the tension had already left my shoulders. Knowing Vincent had already managed this before seemed to relax my muscles.

"Vincent mentioned buying more supplies for it. He wanted to do more lithography. I was not sure what it was. Is it terribly expensive to buy lithography supplies?"

Mr. Zuijderland paused. I could tell that he was contemplating how to answer me.

"Well, yes."

My shoulders tensed again.

"Is it more expensive than drawing supplies?"

"Definitely, it is."

"Is it more expensive than paintings supplies?"

He paused again. His eyes told me that he was contemplating lying to me right then. Mr. Zuijderland could see the worry spreading across my face and was torn between being honest with me and lying to spare my anxiety. He decided on the side of honesty.

"Well, it does depend. From what I understand, if you buy a decent amount of supplies, it can add up to more than painting supplies. It all depends on how much you buy."

My heart sank into my lap. I knew Vincent, and he would buy a great deal of supplies even at the expense of food. His passion for art knew no bounds, and black bread would have to do if he overspent. I looked outside at the air that was getting colder by the day. The window glass even looked cold as the last drops of sunlight danced across it with tiny feet of purple and pink. Vincent was buying more expensive supplies, and winter was nearly here. I thought about the envelopes and how thin they had become of late. I remembered last winter. It was so very cold, and we had been so very hungry.

"Do not fret, Maria. The winter will be short this year. I feel it in my bones."

"I surely hope so."

Chapter Twenty Two

The Hague grew colder and colder the closer we got to Christmas. It was not yet the bitter cold that bit through the skin and into the bones, but we all shivered with every gust of wind. The air smelled sharp and clean, and the people on the streets no longer stopped to chatter with one another about their day. Everyone hurried wherever they went in order to return to their warm hearths as quickly as possible. Moeder helped me make patches for my coat, and Oma knitted a thick baby blanket to bundle little Willem against the chill. The most disheartening part of it all was that this was just the beginning of winter. There would be colder nights and harder times to come. I only hoped we would not run out of food.

I wanted for only two presents on Christmas Day. I normally got nothing in the way of presents on Christmas, aside from the occasional knitted gloves from my Oma. However, this year I had lofty goals. I wanted to eat a meal on Christmas Day. In the past, Moeder might surprise me with a half of a good loaf of bread or even butter if she managed to afford it. This year, I wanted a real meal with meat and everything. I wanted to eat with my family and be warm on Christmas Day. That and I wanted it to snow.

It did snow in The Hague, not very often, but it did happen. The snow never stayed very long, but every once in a while, it would snow and cover the world around us in a powdery white blanket. It was so beautiful when it did happen that I could not help but sit by the window and look at how lovely it was.

Snow had a special magic about it that made everything look clean. The dusty streets, the fish drying house, and the butchery all looked rank and dirty under normal conditions. However, when it snowed, a sparkling white sheen covered the ugly parts of our city

105

and made it look fresh and new. I loved the snow no matter how short lived it always seemed.

Moeder used to ask me why I would not go play in it like the other children.

"They are messing it up. It is too pretty to bat around like idiot kittens," I would reply to her.

She stopped asking me after a time. My answer was always the same.

The day before Christmas, I could tell that my first wish was in jeopardy. We had been forced to eat black bread soaked in water again for breakfast, and no new envelopes had arrived with money from Vincent's family. I looked to Moeder for some reassurance that we were only eating bad food now to save up enough for a feast tomorrow, but she refused to look up from her breakfast. The table was full of quiet, solemn people. I began to fear the worst.

That night, I overheard Sien and Vincent talking in the kitchen.

"What shall we do, Vincent? Would you have us eat black bread and coffee for Christmas dinner?"

"No, I do not wish that, but I have not received the letter from Theo that I have been expecting. Surely he would not abandon us so on Christmas."

"He has abandoned us. I suspect that the mail service will be taking tomorrow as a holiday. We have no money to buy food tomorrow."

"I do not know what you want from me."

"To *feed* us, Vincent."

"I have nothing to offer you but my love, Sien."

"We cannot feast on your love," she retorted.

Silence crept into the room and pulled up a chair for a nice long visit. He replaced the sound of arguing with the uncomfortable buzz of nothing. In fact, he stayed so long that the grumbling in my belly ceased, and I drifted away to sleep. Dreams of silent demons sitting at empty tables haunted my rest all night long.

I awoke late in the morning on Christmas, and my body did not want to rise. I had slept all night, yet it felt like I had been running through a forest instead. My muscles ached and my eyelids were heavy. I smelled the coffee brewing in the kitchen, and the coo of Little Willem. Everyone was awake except me.

I arose in a begrudging manner and stumbled from my bed. The kitchen was bright, and Vincent sat at the table playing with Willem in his lap. He flashed me a cheerful grin. Something had changed for his face lit up with happiness.

"There is my Little Cat. Did you sleep enough?"

"No. It should have been enough, but it was not."

"That is too bad. Have a seat."

I did so and noticed the barren table.

"Is there nothing to eat?"

"Not yet, but there will be," he remarked with a wink.

I squinted at him with a skeptical eye. Had Vincent lost his mind?

"Do not look so cross, Little Cat. Your moeder will be returning with breakfast shortly."

I eyed her empty place at the table.

"Did you get an envelope from your brother?"

His smile faded, and he concentrated his attention back to Willem. It was difficult to look upset while watching the baby. His cheeky smile was impossible to resist even on the worst days.

"No, I did not. I expect one any day now."

I huffed a lungful of air at him.

"Then, how are we to eat today? Where is Moeder?"

Just then, the door open, and Sien entered through the door along with a gust of cold air. I tucked myself into a ball to protect against the chill. She shut the door quickly and immediately removed her head scarf. Her long, dark hair fell down her back as she stared intently at Vincent.

Vincent had stood when she entered, expectedly awaiting something. As soon as he saw her long hair, his face dropped with disappointment. He sank back down into his chair and hugged Willem tighter. A frown plastered itself across his face.

"What happened?" he asked under his breath. "Were they not open today?"

Sien sighed and sat down next to him.

"No, they were open. I was not the only one there trying to sell for their Christmas dinner."

She reached her hand across the table, and he grabbed for it.

"What happened then?"

Tears filled Sien's eyes, and she began to sniffle. She wiped her nose violently with her hand.

"What is happening?" I asked to the two of them. "It is idiotic that you have not told me. What are you talking about?"

"Your moeder, she went to the wig makers shop this morning."

"The wig makers shop? Why there?"

"To sell my hair," said Sien while a few more tears rolled down her cheeks.

We were all quiet for a moment while I pieced this together.

"So, you were going to sell your hair for money?"

"Yes."

"And you did not because…?"

Sien began to weep harder, and she collapsed into her own arms. Her words came out in gasping sobs.

"He said that my hair was not of a fine enough quality. It was too dry, too brittle. He said that it was not good enough for a wig."

It was true that her hair was often a sad mess on top of her head. Her dark hair was brittle and dry. Occasionally, I would brush her hair for her and bits always fell off into my hands. Vincent said that her abuse of the bottle made it worse than it would have been if she were sober.

"He would not take it even for a cheaper price?" asked Vincent.

Sien sniffled beneath her arms.

"He said that he could do better with horse hair. Mine was not worth the price of the barber."

We all sighed and looked at the empty table in front of us in silence. Sien continued to sniffle while she tried to compose herself and end her tears.

"What shall we eat now?" asked Sien to no one in particular.

No one had an answer for her. We just looked at one another without knowing what to say. To add insult to injury, my stomach growled loud enough for everyone to hear.

"Well," began Vincent, "perhaps we could try another wig maker. Surely there is more than one in this city."

Sien exploded out of her chair, all of her sadness suddenly turning to rage.

"You would put me through that humiliation again? I was nearly laughed out of the shop, and you want to me to put myself through that again?"

She was shouting, and it was such a sudden thing that we all jumped in our seats. Willem began to whimper in Vincent's lap.

"Do not scream at me. Had you taken care of yourself, your hair would not be so undesirable that a wig maker would turn you down."

The insult stung her visibly. Hot anger filled her face.

"Me? You blame me? You are the one who went away to spend all of your money of art supplies. Lithography, or what ever is it called. These precious things are more important than feeding your family."

Vincent stood and returned Sien's angry glare. They continued to yell back and forth like this for a while. Willem began to cry adding more noise to the already cacophonic din in the kitchen. This was ridiculous. I was watching my perfect Christmas present slipping away from me right before my eyes.

"Enough!"

Everyone stopped and looked around the room at where the words had originated. Even Willem stopped crying out of shock and confusion. To my own surprise, the word had come from my throat. They stared at me in disbelief.

"I will go to the wig maker and sell my hair."

Shock reverberated through the room, and no one responded to me for a full minute. I barely knew what I had just said. It just came out of my mouth on its own accord. I was standing now, glaring at the both of them.

"Maria, are you sure?" asked Vincent quietly.

"Yes. I have better hair than Moeder. I will do it."

It was true, I had lovely hair. My hair was long and dark brown. It flowed down my back and glistened when the sunlight caught it just so. My hair was as soft and smooth as Sien's was dry and ratted. The wig man would definitely buy my hair.

I stood up from the table without a word and went into my room to wash myself and put on one of my decent dresses. I dressed slowly for I was in no hurry to do this deed. I took great care in every detail of my appearance. Slowly, as if by ritual, I buttoned each button and smoothed all creases. When I was dressed, I sat on my bed combing my hair as though it were a precious thing. I never realized just how precious until I agreed to sell it.

I had never fussed with my hair very much in the past. Normally, I would only run a comb through it quickly before I ran off to do whatever needed to be done. Not today. Today, I sat on the edge of my mattress and slowly ran my comb through my long locks. I gently stroked the part I had just combed through, looking for bits of grass or imperfections. Carefully, I removed any nits or twigs that had taken up residence in my mane without my knowing.

I took the scented oil bottle Oma had given me for my birthday and added a few droplets to the teeth of my comb. The extra oil on my fingers went to my crown where I meticulously slicked every stray fly away hair into its perfect place. Then, I combed through it all again with the oil slicked comb to give my hair that summer sheen it normally only held in the sunlight.

It was a very long process. I did not mind, and I refused to make excuses for how long it all took me. I was saying good bye to my hair, and they would just have to wait.

*   *   *

"This is of a fine quality," said the wig maker after he had inspected my locks.

"Thank you, sir."

Vincent responded for me as I would not say a word to either of them. Sien, too embarrassed to be seen in the shop again, had stayed home with Willem.

"Let us settle the particulars together in the other room while my barber does his work."

Vincent agreed. He gave me one last look before he followed the man into the other room. I could only imagine that the look was one of apology, but I refused to ponder it.

The barber was a young man with a kind look to him. His round face sat strangely on his thin frame. He approached me from my left side and walked all around me with a studying eye.

"Hello," he offered in a friendly way.

"Hello," I offered back.

He pulled out a comb and brushed it through my hair while taking great care not to pull too hard. His hands were sweet and gentle. I wanted to thank him for that, but I said nothing. The barber grabbed my hair and pulled it back to the nape of my neck where he tied it with a bit of leather. I watched him as he walked over to a nearby table and collected a pair of shiny scissors. They glistened in the light from the winter sky that crept in from the adjacent window. My breath caught in my lungs at the sight. It all was becoming more real all of the sudden.

111

"Will it hurt?"

The barber walked back over to me and turned my face away from him.

"Not physically. Are you sure you want to do this?"

I nodded quickly for fear that I would not answer properly if I gave myself time to think about it longer. He placed two large, gentle hands on my shoulders. They were warm and soothing.

"Exhale that breath you are holding."

I did as I was told, and I took two more fast breaths. I hadn't realized I had been holding my breath in like that. My heart was pounding.

"Good. Now, take a deep breath in for me."

I did just as he asked.

"Good, very good. Now, I want you to let it out very slowly."

I let the air leak ever so slowly from my lungs as he had instructed. He removed his right hand from my shoulder and brought the scissors to the back of my head. Before I had finished releasing all of my air, he cut right through the hair bundle he had made. It was done; it was over. In an instant, he had done it. I turned around to see him smiling and holding a fistful of my precious hair.

Chapter Twenty Three

Vincent and I walked home in silence. The world seemed sharper, and the air smelled like how apples tasted, crisp and spiced by nature. Relentless winds whipped our clothes around. The winter chill felt extra cold without my hair to protect my neck. The barber had been good enough to wrap my bonnet for me in a way that made my new haircut less noticeable. I tried not to sulk.

"The wig man gave me quite the price," Vincent offered in a reassuring way.

I said nothing in return. He did not deserve my words as far as I was concerned.

"We will be able to have a great feast tonight. I plan to buy a duck."

I still said nothing.

We kept walking along without a word. I began to think paranoid thoughts. An older woman looked at my head, and I cowered beneath her stare. A girl a little older than me tugged at her own bonnet when she saw me pass by. I suddenly wished that I had a hood to cover my head with. It felt like every person we passed was staring at my lack of hair. I knew the lunacy of this idea, but it felt that way nonetheless. Paranoia was soaking into my very bones.

When Vincent and I reached our apartment, I had never been so relieved to be home. I wanted nothing more than to crawl into my bed, assemble the cushion cave my Oma had made for me, and sleep until supper. I reached for the door, but Vincent stopped me with a hand on my shoulder.

"Sien invited your Oma for dinner tonight. Will that not be fun? We will have the family together for a good meal."

I stared at him with a blank expression.

"Be happy, Little Cat. We will have roasted duck and potatoes this very evening. I might even buy a jug of wine to celebrate the holiday."

He smiled at me with a heart filled with good intentions, but I could not return the sentiment. I was glad Oma was coming for a visit, but what would she think when she saw me this way? My short hair was a huge beacon shining in the night to tell anyone who cared to look just how poor and hungry we were. I sighed and walked into the house, trying to comfort myself with visions of roasted duck and potatoes.

*   *   *

Christmas evening found our little home warm and smelling of food. Vincent had indeed bought a duck, and Moeder had it roasting by the stove fire. Potatoes were boiling away in a pot, and fresh bread and butter was on the table. Soft cheese, salt, and wine were also out for everyone to enjoy. I was slightly overwhelmed by the entire feast. It was hard to stay cross when the air smelled so divinely of food, and I attempted to take heart that at least one of my Christmas presents was going happen for me.

Sien eyed me while I set the table. She had held back her tears earlier when she saw me come home. I removed my bonnet to show her my bare head and hacked haircut. To her credit, those tears were there, but she held them from me with a reasonable amount of grace. Sien even combed what was left for me and styled it in a boyish fashion that did not look terrible.

I offered my moeder a smile, but it was half-hearted. Sometimes pretending to be happy eventually makes one happier, so I continued the ruse. Perhaps when we began eating, I would cheer. The food smelled wonderful after all.

Vincent joined us in the kitchen with Willem just in time to hear the light knocking at our door. We all went to answer it, knowing who it was and wishing to greet her in a holiday fashion. Moeder opened the door to reveal Oma standing in the cold and wearing two extra shawls to keep the biting chill away. In her hands, she held what looked like a stack of sweet pancakes. My mouth watered just looking at them.

"Welcome, Moeder!" exclaimed Sien motioning for Oma to enter.

She smiled at Sien and Vincent. Little Willem giggled on Sien's hip at the sight of his Oma, and she tickled at his belly. Oma had not seen me yet. I was slightly behind Moeder's skirt. She had to step into the threshold of the apartment to see me. When she did, she froze in her place.

I looked up at her and tried for a happy smile to tell her it was all going to be fine. I was trying to say so much in that one smile. I wanted her to know that I had no choice and that everything would be alright. My smile must have shown through false because a look of disgust crossed her face like I had not seen.

"What is the meaning of this, Sien?"

The mood in the apartment changed in an instant. Food still permeated the air, but the smell suddenly seemed rotten and foul. I swallowed a large lump that kept sticking in my throat.

"What do you mean, Moeder?"

"Do not act dumb with me, child. What has happened to Maria's hair?"

Sien recoiled in fear. Oma's voice was now angry. I was used to her stern voice. She was an honest woman who never minced words, but now she was angry. I tried to memorize the tone. If I had ever needed to be taken seriously, I would use that tone.

"It is not such a terrible thing," interjected Vincent. "Maria volunteered it. She was kind enough to do this so that we may have this wonderful Christmas feast."

Oma turned her glare on him.

"You mean that you could not provide for this family on Christmas, so you allowed a child to do so?"

Her words came out as though she were spitting at him.

"Moeder, please. I tried to do it myself, but they would not take my hair."

Oma eyed her daughter with contempt, and then she looked at me.

"Maria, did you agree to this?"

I nodded solemnly. I felt like I was admitting someone else's wrong doing, but I shared in the guilt somehow. Lies were never my forte, so I told her the truth.

"We were hungry, and there was no other way."

Oma softened her look at me and sighed. Then, she looked at Vincent and Sien with hatred in her eyes.

"I will take no part in this dinner. Shame on the both of you!"

She turned on her heel, and walked out of the door in a hurry. I ran after her in a panic, calling her name and begging for her to stop. Thankfully, she stopped when she reached the street and turned to face me.

"Go back inside, Maria. It is cold, and you have no bonnet."

"It will grow back," I said breathlessly.

"What?"

"The barber said that it will grow back. Please come back in and eat with us."

"I cannot. They have disgusted me, but you should take this."

She handed me the platter of dessert pancakes, and I took them. The cold of the ceramic stung my fingers like ice.

"They are for you and no one else. You are the only one who deserves them."

She stormed off into the night then. I could hear her mutter curses under her breath as she walked away. I called out to her again, but the wind carried them back to me as it whirled around, chilling my neck where my hair had once been. I was alone in the quiet darkness of the Christmas Eve.

Suddenly, I felt something wet and cold land on my nose. It was delicate but unmistakable. Another one settled tenderly on my right forearm and melted away on my skin into a tiny puddle. Yet another floated its way to my left knuckle and kissed it once before it vanished. I looked up to the heavens and saw that snow was falling down all around me. The flakes danced about the sky like tiny cherubs falling in billowy clouds. It smelled sweetly of cold as I raised my head back and opened my mouth. I caught several on my tongue, and they tasted like small pinpricks of cold.

Both of my Christmas wishes had come true.

Chapter Twenty Four

After Christmas, Sien was ashamed and rarely spoke to any of us for a long amount of time. Her drinking worsened, but only I seemed to notice the change in her. It was like the old, bad days except worse. There had still been money left over from when they sold my hair. I watched as the sum dwindled away from Sien's thievery. Vincent hardly noticed any of this. He chose to vent his own shame in his studio. He, too, barely spoke to anyone, but it was for different reasons. Vincent was in one of his concentrated states, and he cared little for everyone else.

One evening, Sien drank herself to the point of unconsciousness. I found her only because I had heard a loud noise in her room like someone dropping a bundle of laundry. Vincent was still working in his studio, so I crept into their room to see if everything was all right.

I found her collapsed on the floor by the foot of the bed. She looked like a large bundle of clothes waiting for someone to launder them. I ran to her side and checked her chest. It rose and fell noticeably with her every breath. I relaxed knowing that she was alive.

I tried to lift her body in an attempt to put her to bed, but she was far too heavy for my small arms to manage. I rolled her over on her back, and she snored and sputtered with each breath. When I was younger, I used to slap her face to wake her from stupors like this, but when I struck her this time, she did not rouse at all. Her face only moved under the force of each blow. Once, her eyes opened and lolled in their sockets for a moment before she fell back to sleep, but that was the only response I got.

This was obviously a hopeless task on my own, and I did not dare disturb Vincent in his current mood. I could not lift her to the bed myself, and I could not leave her here to freeze, exposed to the chill of the night. A compromise was in order.

I removed a pillow from their bed and placed it under Moeder's head. Then, I dragged their blankets off the mattress. I covered Sien from head to toe with the blankets and tucked them around her body as well as I could. When the work was done, I stood back to survey my handiwork. She looked like a pastry made of fabric, but it would work. Sien may have to spend a night on the hard floor, but at least she would be warm. I resigned that that was the best I could manage for her, and I went to my own room to sleep.

I could not have been asleep more than a few minutes when I heard Willem begin to cry. I released a long, exhausted breath. Sien would never wake from her stupor. My only chance for peace that night was if Vincent helped the baby. I thought that there was a good chance that he might since little Willem was in the studio with him. Surely the sound would disturb him so that he had to do something.

I laid in my room listening to the sounds of Willem screaming for a while, hoping Vincent would attend to him, and I could go to sleep. Maybe he would cry himself back to sleep. I tried to muffle the sound of the cries by putting my hands over my ears but to no avail. The sound of a baby's wailing could pierce through almost anything. There seemed to be no sign of it desisting any time soon, so I rose and resigned to fact that I would have to attend to Willem myself in order to get any sleep that night.

I found Vincent in the studio working by lantern light at his desk. He was in the very same room as the child and never so much as turned around to look at him. I exhaled an annoyed breath loud enough for him to hear before I went over to Willem's basinet. I would have done my Little Cat routine, but I wanted him to hear me this time. The baby was red faced and balling as I pulled back the curtain that marked off his room. He became even more agitated when he saw me, and he squirmed and wriggled in his basinet. Willem reached for me as I neared him, and as soon as I took him in my arms, I could feel that he was wet.

I changed his clothes with fresh ones, and he began to quiet while I bounced him against my shoulder and patted his back. A large belch erupted from his body, and Willem relaxed completely into my arms. It was not long before I felt the heady cadence of his infant's breath fall rhythmically on my shoulder. We both breathed relief into each others' hair. I laid him down in his basinet with great care so as not to wake him. With one hand, I gently rocked his basinet until his body completely relaxed.

At last, I thought I would finally be able to go to bed. The mattress seemed to be calling to me from the other room. However, when I turned around, I saw Vincent staring at me and Willem. His eyes were wild and blood shot from lack of sleep. He had fresh paper and charcoal in hand.

"That was beautiful. Truly lovely," he whispered.

I rubbed my tired eyes and stared at him.

"I just changed him," I whispered back.

"Yes, but it is the two of you. You are both filled with such love for each other. I have to draw you both, right now."

He had the manic look of the insistent in his eyes, and I blinked hard, thinking that I heard him wrong.

"You want to draw us now? You want to wake him up again?"

I sounded incredulous.

"No, he can stay asleep. Just kneel by his basinet like you were."

I turned away from Vincent, and did as he instructed. Exhaustion seemed to have robbed me of the ability to do anything else but obey. It felt like a waking dream. I knelt beside Willem's basinet and placed one hand on the edge of it.

"Perfect! That is perfect. Hold that just as you are."

I was so tired, and my knees ached from kneeling on the hard floor. Every time my shoulders began to slump, my back would whine in protest, and I would have to correct myself upright. My eyes were heavy, and all I wanted was to go back to bed. I thought about protesting and leaving the studio, but my will power had left me. Besides, no one could argue with Vincent as he was right now. He would just insist until I did what he wanted from me.

Meanwhile, I could hear the scratching of charcoal to paper behind me. The sound was feverishly fast. I wondered if he was wearing a hole in the paper at that pace. Vincent rambled on to me in a manic whisper. Half of it sounded like the words of the insane. I could barely understand what he said. Some of it was comprehensible, so I tried to focus on those bits in order to stay awake. I was just glad he was whispering so he did not wake Willem again.

"You know that your moeder is stupid."

It was not a question, merely a statement of something we both knew to be true.

"She knows nothing of books or art. She is of the ignorant majority. Sien never really knows what she speaks of when she tries to speak of anything."

I said nothing. What was there to say?

"Daumier would love her. He is a master of capturing the common man. He prefers the idiot masses to the learned bourgeois. The masses have so much more soul to them. The sorrow and turmoil in their lives is palpable in Daumier's drawings. Every line depicts struggle and despair. What a master! He would have loved to have your moeder model for him. She is just the correct type, stupid and wrong in the correct ways of society."

I sighed and hoped this session would be over soon. The only thing worse than Vincent in an intense mood of concentration was Vincent concentrating intensely on you. He seemed to take no notice that I was tired and needed to rest.

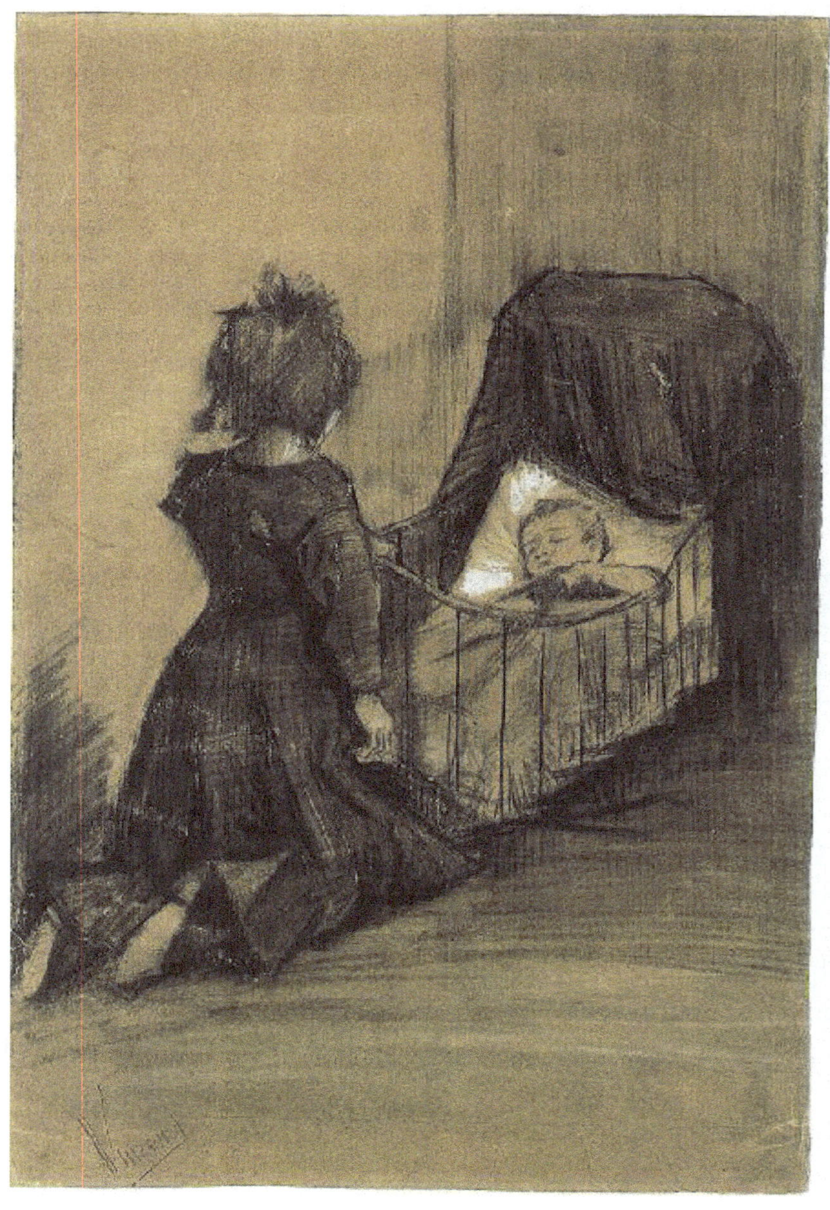

"Daumier, he is the key. He is a man from which to learn the secrets of the soul. The common folk are the key. Yes, Daumier is the right path. That is a certainty. There can be no argument there."

I was unsure who Daumier was. I remembered Vincent speaking of him before, but it was when he was normal and speaking intelligently. He was an artist Vincent admired, that was certain. Whoever this Daumier was, I made a pact with myself to never be the type of person he loved to draw.

Chapter Twenty Five

I came across one of Vincent's unfinished letters to his brother Theo purely by accident one afternoon. Vincent was sleeping in his bedroom since he had been awake most the night drawing and painting, and I was trying to tidy his desk. My ulterior motives were not to spy on the man's correspondence but to simply relocate Victor Hugo's book before Mr. Zuijderland came to visit. I happened to find the allusive book only when I lifted Vincent's unfinished letter.

Now that my lessons had progressed so well, I took the time to try to read the letter myself. I did not think the act would be so terrible, but I also did not want Vincent to catch me. I quietly shut the door and read what I could. To my surprise, Vincent was describing our family to his brother. Some words looked to be about me, but there were quite a few words that I did not know. The suspense of wanting to know what Vincent wrote about me was thrilling and terrible, but I could not understand much of what was written. I decided to wait for Mr. Zuijderland to arrive in the hopes that he would help me. He did so an hour later, and I greeted him at the door.

"Hello there, Maria. How are you today?"

"Well, Mr. Zuijderland. Thank you. How are you?"

"Well. I have not suffocated from the air of the old people just as yet, so I have nothing much to complain about."

He smiled at me, and I smiled back. I loved his company.

"Is Vincent ready for me today?"

"He was awake all night working. I am afraid that he is asleep now."

"Oh well, you look awake. Shall we work on your reading, Little Cat?"

I nodded emphatically and handed him some coffee I had made in anticipation of his arrival. Vincent, Moeder, and Willem were sleeping, so we had the house to ourselves. He thanked me, and we retired to the studio. The sky was overcast with only a grey light shining in through the window. Mr. Zuijderland and I had to huddle together at the desk in order to see what we were doing. We made new words with the letters I knew, and he made me speak the words aloud. I hated that part. I much preferred to read in silence, but he said that he could not read what I was reading in my head. How was he to know if I was reading correctly? So, I read them aloud as he watched.

My lessons went as they always did, but I was restless this day. I had been waiting for the perfect time to ask the old man to help me read Vincent's letter, but it had not presented itself. I fidgeted noticeably in my chair, and Mr. Zuijderland asked me about it.

"Is there something wrong with your seat, Maria?"

"No, sir."

"Then why do you bounce so?"

I took a deep breath and let it out blowing a few of the papers away from us.

"I have a favor to ask of you, but I do not know if you will consent."

"Well, if I never know what the favor is, how may I consent? You had better ask me to be sure before you wear a hole in your chair."

I shifted in my seat again and pulled out the unfinished letter Vincent had written. Mr. Zuijderland took it out and eyed me skeptically.

"Would you read this to me? Or could you help me read it?"

He stretched out his arm as far as it could reach and the read the words at the end of his hand. Mr. Zuijderland often read this way, and I thought it was a funny sort of tradition of his. How anyone read that far away from the words I would never know.

"This is a private correspondence. Where did you get this?"

He sounded a little suspicious, and I shrank in my seat.

"I found it here on the desk."

"Why do you want me to read it?"

"It is about me, I believe."

Mr. Zuijderland nodded.

"Yes, a part of it is about you, but this is Vincent's private letter. I am not sure that we should use it to read."

"Well, it was not kept as a secret," I said in a small voice.

"What do you mean?"

"It was laying out on the desk, not hidden in a drawer. There was no lock and key. The letter was out in the open for all to see."

"Maybe Vincent was not worried about people in this house reading it because he knows your moeder cannot read."

"He does not know that I cannot read. It must not be such a secret if he left if in the open for anyone to find, including me."

Mr. Zuijderland shook his head.

"I do not know, Maria. Perhaps you should put this back where you found it."

I huffed and felt my face go red. How would I ever know what Vincent had to say about me if Mr. Zuijderland did not help me now? Soon, Vincent would finish his letter and send it away. I would never know then. I puffed out my chest, sat up as straight as I could manage, and looked the old man in the eyes.

"Mr. Zuijderland, this letter is about me, and I think I have a right to know what Vincent is saying about me to a stranger."

He looked taken aback for a moment. I wondered desperately what was going through his mind. My tone was meant to land on the side of determined, but I worried that I had crossed over to the side of insulting. He finally smiled a little at me, and I relaxed.

"You have a point. Do not tell Vincent that you and I read his letter. That will have to be our little secret."

I agreed.

"Are you sure you want to hear this? Sometimes hearing what people say about you when you are not there to defend yourself can be a little jarring."

"I want to know," I replied with my determined voice again. It had worked for me before.

He nodded.

"I will only read the part that is about you and your family."

Mr. Zuijderland gazed down at the paper and began to read.

"At this moment the woman and the children are sitting with me. When I think of last year, there is a great difference. The woman is stronger and stouter, has lost much of her agitated air. The baby is the prettiest, healthiest, merriest little fellow you can imagine. And the poor little girl…"

He trailed off then and looked at me over the paper. I knew this part was about me. I signaled to him to keep going.

"…you see from the drawings that her former deep misery has not been wiped out, and I often feel anxious about her. But still, she is quite different from last year. Then, she was in a very bad state; now, she is already looking more childlike. I feel like she might yet be saved from this world after all."

The old man put the paper on the desk, and looked at me. He had been correct. Hearing someone speak about me had caused me to feel immediately embarrassed. It was like being exposed. Even though only the two of us were in the room, I felt like a crowd of people had been invited to come in and watch me undress in the privacy of my bedroom. I folded my hands in my lap and stared at him while pondering the words.

"Maria, are you all right?"

I thought long and hard about what those words meant. Vincent often felt anxious about me? It was true that I was very different than I had been last year, but I had grown. I was his friend and confidant. Why should he feel anxious about me? The last part troubled me the worst. Vincent said that I was more childish. Did he really think me childish? The thought made my chest ache.

"Maria? You must speak to me, girl."

I looked up at Mr. Zuijderland.

"Do you think I am childish?"

He smiled down at me.

"Is that what is troubling you? No Maria, I think you are more grown than most adults I know."

"Then why would Vincent say that about me?"

"I do not think he meant it like you mean it. He means that you are not so serious as when he first met you. You have joy in your face like a child would. That is all."

"But, he and I are friends. How can he be friends with someone he sees as a child?"

"Maria, your body is that of a child's, but your heart and mind are not. That is why we are such friends. Your mind is friends with our minds. Vincent is just happy that your body is happier like a child's. Look at little Willem. His is chubby and happy. We should aspire to have our bodies as happy as his."

He put his hand on my head and patted me.

"I would not fret over such things. You have the rest of your life to fret your health away. Be a child while you can."

Chapter Twenty Six

In March, it began to warm a little, and in a way, I think it warmed Vincent towards Sien. He ceased working his insane hours in the studio and tried to focus more attention on her. Vincent insisted on taking her for romantic strolls around the city. The bitterest chill had left The Hague, making a stroll a luxury that was possible again. I offered to stay home with Willem so that they might rekindle their past love with one another on these afternoon jaunts.

At first, Sien seemed to brighten to his sudden affections. The fresh air and attention of her lover filled her with good health and cheer. Soon, the attention became that of a smothering parent as Vincent was able to see first hand what she had been doing to herself these past months while he was working. Many of their walks ended with them arguing as they stormed in our front door.

"You did not seem to mind my habits when you were held up in your studio like a hermit!" spat Sien one day after they had returned from a walk.

I hid in the studio watching them through a crack in the door.

"I had to work, Sien. I could not be disturbed. But I am here now, and I can see what has been happening. You must stop this drinking at once."

"I will do as I like. Besides, I do not drink all that much. You are exaggerating the situation."

"Am I?"

He reached into the pantry and removed a loaf of bread that had been blackened on the bottom side.

"Your children eat this while you spend the money on liquor."

He slammed the bread on the table in a fit of flying black crumbs.

"And you spend our money on art supplies instead of food for all of us. You are just as guilty! If you took a job, we could eat again."

Vincent glared at her.

"If you loved me as you say you do, you would not say such words to me."

He stormed out of the apartment. She marched to their bedroom and slammed the door. This happened more and more until Sien finally just ceded to his demands. She promised Vincent that she would no longer drink. He would again have the dutiful, pious woman that he deserved. Of course, all that meant was that she was more careful in how she drank. She still sneaked bottles in the house, and she drank even more than she had before. The only difference was that she was careful to do it when he was not around.

*   *   *

March thirtieth marked Vincent's birthday, and we had a small party for him. We invited Mr. Zuijderland and my Oma to the gathering at our apartment. I was happy. Our home had been in much need of fun, and what better way to remedy that than to have good friends over to celebrate with us.

Mr. Zuijderland brought some dried meat, and Oma brought some soft cheese. Vincent had negated his normal allowance for charcoal and paper that week in order to buy some fine bread and cheaper wine. Vincent and Mr. Zuijderland smoked their pipes together, and the kitchen was filled with the smell of sweet tobacco. Oma and I played with Willem, and he laughed at us with his entire belly. The mood was light, but there was no sign of Sien.

"Where is your moeder?" whispered Oma to me.

"I do not know. She was napping in her room earlier. I am sure she will join us soon."

Oma nodded.

"Perhaps she is just making herself look presentable."

I nodded back.

Just then, Mr. Zuijderland came over to me and patted my head. He walked me away from Oma and whispered conspiratorially to me.

"How far did you get on that page from the book?"

"One half of the page," I whispered back. "I understand almost all of it."

I smiled at the old man with the strange hair with a great pride. The main part that had been holding back my progress was the difference between names and words. They looked the same to me, and the difference caused me so much confusion. In our last lesson, Mr. Zuijderland explained that words meant something while names were the names we call things, whether it be a person or a city. He said that I could always tell the difference by looking at the first letter of the word. If it was a capital letter, it was probably a name. Such a difference that revelation had made.

Mr. Zuijderland had told me to remember that and try to read the Victor Hugo book again to see how far I could get before I stopped understanding what was being said. I made it through half of the page, and I was very proud.

"Tremendous effort, Maria!"

My eyes widened, and I put my finger to my lips and shushed him playfully.

"Mr. Zuijderland, you will give away our secret," I whispered with a laugh.

He made himself look overly contrite, as he nodded and patted my head again.

"My apologies. I am just so very proud of you."

We all turned when we heard the door to the bedroom creak. At first, I was happy to think that Moeder was finally coming out to join us. Then, we saw her. Her dress hung loosely on her shoulders as it was only half buttoned. A matted bundle of dry hair was knotted on top of her head, swaying uneasily back and forth as she moved. Her eyes were red rimmed and dark with sunken circles underneath them. She breathed heavily like a rabid dog might after chasing his prey. Sien was drunk, very drunk.

I closed my eyes in embarrassment as she stumbled into the kitchen unsteadily. Sien swayed back and forth as though she were a vessel at sea. She nearly fell once but managed to catch herself on the table. A wet belch left her throat.

"Sien, are you all right?" asked my Oma.

She looked horrified at her daughter. Oma had not been to visit us since she walked out on our Christmas dinner. I had visited her, and she had seen Willem, but I did not think she had seen Sien in all that time. Oma was still very upset by what she had seen that night and made no effort to visit with her daughter.

"I am afraid that our poor Sien is sick with fever," said Vincent as he rushed over and lifted her in his arms. "She is a bit delirious from the heat of it. Excuse us, friends. I will replace her in bed."

Vincent carried her away like a pile of rags. She did not fight him.

I looked at Sien and saw her the way Oma probably saw her. She was much thinner than she had been, almost skeletal, really. We had had less food this winter, and times had been rough for us. Moeder had taken extra alcohol to supplement the bread she was not eating. She was a pitiful, drunken sight. She was an impoverished soul. Daumier would have loved her. Oma eyed me from across the room. I knew that she saw the poverty of her daughter and would do something about it.

Chapter Twenty Seven

After the debacle of Vincent's birthday, Sien's condition grew steadily worse. They argued even more than they had before. The lack of money made everything harder than it had to be. Hungry people are quicker to anger.

The house fell quickly into disrepair. Sien rarely rose from her bed, and when she did, she spent a great deal of time at Oma's house with Willem and me. I tried to help with the cleaning, but it was far too much to tackle on my own. When Vincent would chastise Sien for her lack of attention to the apartment, she would only sigh and go back to her bed.

I loved spending afternoons with my Oma, but it became apparent very quickly that Oma had ulterior motives in mind. These were not just visits to spend time with her daughter. They were excuses for her to get Sien alone. Moeder and Oma often left Willem and me to play together in the parlor, bribed with cow's milk, while they whispered secrets in the kitchen to one another.

One afternoon, I decided to be Little Cat. I removed my shoes and left them for Willem to play with while I crept to the door of the kitchen to listen to what they were saying. I was careful not to stand directly in front of the door for my shadow would give me away. A knothole near the side offered me a perfect vantage point for which to spy on them.

Moeder looked tired as always. She was slumped in her chair and holding a cup of coffee. Oma sat upright next to her, sipping from her own cup.

"I do not know, Moeder. Please stop asking me."

"It is a simple question, Sien. How much money does he get from his brother?"

"Again, I do not know. It varies. Sometimes it is more, sometimes it is less. It is never consistent."

"Well, how much does he spend on art supplies?"

"That too varies."

"My God, Sien, sit up!" Oma snapped.

Moeder sat up quickly as though someone stabbed her rear with a fire stick.

"Get a hold of yourself, my girl. Look at you! All bones and skin. Have you seen your daughter? I have seen orphaned children her age with more weight to them. You cannot continue this way. Vincent is a nice man, but he cannot support you. He is far too poor to ever marry you. This is a disgrace. You must collect yourself and feed your children."

"We have been worse before," replied Moeder sadly.

"Yes, when it was you and only you supporting you and Maria. You two barely made it. Now there is Willem. Would you have that innocent boy fall victim to the same fate as your lost children?"

At that, Sien's eyes filled with tears and she began to cry.

"What would you have me do, Moeder? Shall I prostitute myself again?"

Oma placed her hand gingerly on her daughter's hand while she wept.

"I would have you do whatever you must to keep Maria and Willem alive."

*　　　*　　　*

It was a Saturday, and Vincent's nerves were peaked. His father had finally conceded to come for a visit. I had helped him clean our home like we had when Sien brought Willem home from Leiden. Our hands were raw from the exertion. Everything was spotless, and we were both a bundle of anticipation. Sien had not risen from her bed that day, and she did not stir even when a rapping on the front door signaled that our visitor had arrived.

Vincent stared at the front door and back to the door of her room with a panicked look on his face. I came forth from my room dressed in my best dress and my cleanest bonnet. I even put on a pretty shawl that Sien never wore because it was too small for her. Vincent smiled at me and opened the door. We knew that we were going to have to do this without her. I was prepared to receive our guest even if Moeder was not.

"Father," Vincent said greeting the man before him. "I am so pleased you could visit. Please, come in and relax. I am sure your journey was a long one."

Vincent's father was the sturdy type. He was taller than his son and had a looming presence about him that made you realize he was a serious man. His eyes were sharp and piercing like Vincent's, but that was where the similarities ended. The man had nearly white hair that was slicked at the sides and fashioned as though it had been chiseled out of stone. His face had no beard. In fact, his jaw was so precisely clean and sharp it looked as though it could be used to cut through wood. He wore the black suit and stark white shirt of a reverend. I had never seen a tie laced so perfectly. No color adorned his lapel in the form of jewelry of any kind to distract you from the fact that he was a serious man of God. Every hair of this man was intimidating.

I stepped forward no matter how much my mind screamed for me to run away. Vincent smiled at me and moved to my side.

"Father, this is Sien's daughter, Maria. She is quite the little art critic."

The serious man looked down at me. It felt like those eyes could see right through my skin and read every lie I ever uttered. I struggled not to back away.

"Hello, Reverend van Gogh. I am Maria Hoornik. Welcome to our home."

I had practiced that greeting all day with Vincent. He nodded at me.

"Good day to you, Maria."

I smiled and we walked together into the kitchen.

"Sien is feeling ill, I am afraid." said Vincent apologetically. "She is sleeping, but I have made some coffee for us to enjoy here in the kitchen."

The reverend walked around the kitchen eyeing everything with a probing glare. Even though we had cleaned, the man still looked around as if he had walked into filthiest sort of brothel and did not know where to sit. After an insufferable amount of time of him inspecting everything, he sat at the table with Vincent. Coffee was served. As they sipped their cups of coffee, Vincent smiled like an idiot, not knowing what else to do. The reverend said nothing and continued to look around the room as though a hoard of insects were crawling up the walls.

Just then, Willem cried from the studio. He was waking from his nap and needed to be changed. I thanked God for his timing. The uncomfortable silence in the kitchen had become too much for me to bear gracefully.

"What baby is that?"

"That is Sien's son I told you about. He is quite the charming little fellow."

"I will go tend to him," I said quickly and hurried out of the kitchen.

As soon as the studio door shut behind me, I felt as if I could breathe again. I could not imagine growing up with such an unpleasant man. I walked over to Willem's basinet and thanked him in a whisper for choosing that moment to wet himself.

"Thank you, little Willem. I needed someone to save me."

He gurgled some spittle at me in response.

After changing the baby, I collected him in my arms and headed to the kitchen. Even the surliest person had a difficult time frowning around Willem. He was the best sort of medicine for all situations.

I returned to the kitchen to find the reverend standing by the table. Vincent was begging him not to go. Only a small amount of coffee had been drunk, and I had not heard any signs of an argument. I approached them looking perplexed. Reverend van Gogh saw me holding the baby and turned back to his son.

"Vincent, you have truly taken leave of your senses. I will not stand here and pretend that this is not the farce that it is. I do not care how much you wish it."

The serious man then left our home and disappeared into an awaiting carriage. Vincent followed him out into the street, begging for him to understand and to stay. It was no use. His words were lost to the whinnying of the horses and the squeaking of the carriage wheels. In a matter of moments, the severe man was gone.

I joined Vincent outside with Willem on my hip. The infant kicked and cooed at the colors of the clouds as twilight began to fall gently over The Hague. It lit up Vincent's forlorn face with hues of purple. The color looked pretty despite everything that had just happened. It was as if the sky knew we had failed, and it was painting everything lovely to cheer us up.

I tugged on his jacket, and he looked down at me.

"I did not do it right, did I? I got something wrong?"

He smiled his sad smile at me. A world of melancholy floated in his eyes.

"No, Little Cat. This was not your fault. It was mine."

Chapter Twenty Eight

"Sien, you will rise from that bed and speak to me!"

Vincent's angry voice could be heard throughout the apartment even with his bedroom door shut. I flipped over on my stomach and covered my head with my pillow to drown out the noise. This had been happening every night since his father had stormed out of our home. A dark cloud hovered over our unhappy lives.

"Leave me alone, Vincent."

"I will not. Sit up and get out of bed. Or are you too drunk to stand?"

Sien let out a huge gust of air.

"What business is it of yours?"

"You promised me, Sien. Do you not remember the promise that you made to live a more pious life with me?"

There was a long silence.

"I am sorry, Vincent. I have broken my promise to you. It must be the hunger pangs; they have caused me to lose my head."

I winced into my pillow. The sarcasm in her voice was as thick as cream. This one was not going to end quickly.

"Why do you speak to me with such disdain? What have I done to merit your scorn?"

Sien did not respond.

"It is your moeder, is it not? She has been whispering poison into your ears. What is she saying to you? You must tell me."

"She says nothing that I do not already tell myself."

There was another pause between them. I wished that I could block out the words somehow. I tried shoving the cloth from one of my bonnets in my ears. No part of me wanted to hear this.

"Oh, and what are those words? Pray tell me, Sien."

I imagined Moeder sitting up in their bed, eyes heavy with drink and dizzy from sleep. Her dress was probably only half fastened, and I could picture the rat's nest that was the pile of hair on her head. Her voice was slightly slurred; I could hear it.

I pictured Vincent pacing about the room in a rage that could not be soothed. His hair would be messed from his frustrated habit of running his hands through it over and over again. This was all so routine these days, I did not even have to see the scene to picture it perfectly in my mind.

Would Sien actually tell him what she and Oma had discussed, or would she placate him again until it was time for another argument? Would this just end in another series of lies and empty promises? At that point, my only hope was that they did not wake up Willem with their shouting.

"Moeder suggested that I go to work for Pieter, keeping house for him. She already goes there occasionally to clean. She can always use extra money, and so could we. I think I should do it. We would be able to have more money for food."

"Pieter! You mean that wretched brother of yours? Absolutely not, Sien!"

"I do not like the idea either, but it is better than going back to the street."

A heady pause overtook the entire house. That storm cloud ceased its raining long enough to encompass us all with the humidity of unspoken words. Moeder's prostitution was a subject not often visited around Vincent. His feelings about it were well known to everyone.

"These are the whisperings that come from your moeder," he said at last. "I was correct, they are poison."

"Vincent, we must eat!"

"So, you would go to your evil brother's home. You know that he divorced his wife. And if divorcing her was not scandalous enough, he beat the poor woman senseless before he abandoned her.

I hear he now keeps a mistress who runs a brothel. Perhaps a woman such as that will last longer in the company of your brother than his pious wife had. And you want to go tend to his house for money?"

"I know the stories of Pieter better than anyone. I am not ignorant to his ways. I said that it is not an ideal plan."

"And the other idea is to go back to the street and sell yourself? You wish to debase your soul by selling your body to strangers after I saved you from that life?"

"No!" shrieked Sien exasperated by the fight. "I want none of it, Vincent, but I would do it if I had to! I would do it to feed my children!"

I was holding my breath as silence crept into their bedroom. The air was rank with all of the words unsaid and all of the words that could never be retrieved. I wondered what would happen now. Surely, Sien would not go back to streets. A tear formed in my eye at the thought.

"What other poison has your moeder been filling your head with?"

"She says that you are too poor to support us and that you will never marry me. She says that I must do something or we will starve when you leave us someday, penniless and destitute."

How I wished that what Sien said was not true. I wanted to think that Oma would never say such a thing, but the truth was undeniable. I had heard it myself.

"Sien," began Vincent with in a quieter tone. "I will not have you go to Pieter's house and disgrace yourself in his presence. I know the stories you have told me about the evil boy you grew up with, and I refuse to send you to that monster."

I could hear that Moeder had started crying.

"I also do not want you to debase yourself by returning to your former life. It is a practice that is beneath you, no matter what your moeder says."

"But Vincent, what shall we do? How will we live?"

"We will find a way, Sien. I promise you that if you cast your former life aside and vow never to return to it, I will never leave you. We will make a life together as a family. If you ever go back to that life, I cannot promise you anything."

Sien sniffled on the other side of the door.

"And, I think that it is time we cast aside your family."

My heart stopped for a moment and fell into my feet.

"What? Vincent, what do you mean?"

"I mean that they have turned poisonous, especially your moeder. I do not want you visiting her any longer. She will only be invited here for special occasions. She is a poor influence on you, and we need to make you well on your road to virtue. The road to piety is often plagued with pressure from the wicked."

I forced my hands over my mouth to conceal my gasp. He could not possibly take my Oma away. Not her.

"But, Vincent, I think that is a bit harsh. I cannot simply stay away from my moeder. Besides, what about Maria? She loves seeing her Oma."

"Maria can visit her from time to time. She is a stubborn girl, and I do not worry about your moeder influencing her as much as you. You are in a fragile state now. We must keep all poisonous talk away from you."

I breathed a sigh of relief at the mention of me. At least, I would still be able to see her sometime, but the horror of disowning Oma was still causing my body to shake.

"Say that you promise you will do all of these things for me. No more talk of your former life. You will put all of that aside, and you will stay away from your moeder. It will be wonderful, Sien. You and I shall walk the path of the pious together, and, someday, I will earn enough money to marry you. Imagine how happy we will be. All you have to do is promise me."

She paused for a while.

"Perhaps this life is truly a farce. Maybe it would be better to end it now. If I cannot feed my children and see my moeder, what is the point of living?"

"What do you mean by that, Sien? Are you truly talking about the sin of suicide right now? How could you when we are so close to leading a truly holy life together as a real family? Surely, you would not abandon us now when we are so close."

I heard her take a long, labored breath.

"No, of course not. I do not know what I could have been thinking. Forgive me, Vincent."

Her words sounded bland and metallic. They were the correct words but without the meaning. Vincent pressed further, undaunted by her sudden lack of depth.

"Then promise me, Sien. Promise me, and be the strong woman I know you can be."

Sien said nothing for a while, and all three of us sat in anticipation for her answer. Would she forsake her old life and her own moeder for Vincent? A betting woman I was not, so I sat in suspense.

"All right, Vincent. I promise this to you. I shall do what you ask."

At that moment, little Willem began to wail in the other room. Perhaps he had been waiting to hear her answer as well.

<h1 style="text-align:center">Chapter Twenty Nine</h1>

Two weeks later, a package came to the apartment from Vincent's parents. We were all surprised and thrilled by its arrival. It was larger than the last parcel, and Vincent was not able to lift it easily on the table this time. He cut the string with a joyous smile on his face and opened the box like we had won a great prize.

The package contained a box of cigars, a hat, a cake, and a white envelope with money and a letter. We were overjoyed. Apparently, his father had not forsaken us as we had thought. The smell of the cake made all of us salivate with hunger. I could not remember when the last time was that I had eaten cake, especially not one that looked as fine as this one.

"Ah, Maria, look here," said Vincent as he pulled out a black garment from the depths of the box.

He presented to me a beautiful black coat that was a perfect size for me. I had been using old coats of Sien's that were too small for her, and they fit terribly. They hung loose and big on my small body like a grain sack only half full. This one looked like it was made for me, and I eyed it in wonder.

"I believe you made an impression," he said smiling.

He handed me the coat. I held it like it was a precious treasure. Never had I received something so fine that was meant for only me.

We decided to eat the cake right then to celebrate. The cake was small, so Moeder sliced it in three segments. We were all given equal shares to enjoy. Vincent and Sien ate theirs entirely right away. I ate half, and, even though my belly rumbled and wanted more, I wrapped the other half in paper and hid it in my room. I wanted to save it for a time when I really needed it.

Vincent made a show of putting the money out on the table in order for Sien to see it. The amount was not so much, but her sunken eyes lit up when she gazed at the coins spread out before her. I could not help but wonder if this money would go to food, her alcohol, or his art supplies. My belly hoped for food.

I looked at the letter Vincent had in front of him. He had read it quickly then let it fall to the table. No expression of his divulged the content of the letter. As I peered around him at the writing, my first reaction was that it was an awfully short letter. A steady scrawl of letters filled the page only halfway. Most of the letter was too obscured by Vincent's hand to read, but a postscript was visible that I managed to understand.

This will be the last letter you receive from me until you correct your life. No longer will we finance this one.

I looked up quickly to see Vincent staring down at me. He saw the recognition in my face and placed his finger over his lips. Silence was what he requested. He did not want Sien to know.

I was horrified, but I tried to mask my face. These gifts were parting gifts. His father did not want to seem a monster, so he sent us some money and a cake. No more white envelopes would come along to save us from starvation. We could count no longer on the charity of his parents. They disapproved of his whore, and now, they had abandoned us. I could not help but wonder how long it would take Theo to do the same.

Sien was oblivious to our current masked state of panic. I said nothing while we watched her count the coins on the table. Little Willem whimpered in the studio and then began crying. I had learned what each of his cries meant long ago, and this was a hungry cry. Moeder stood up from the table and went to the studio to feed him, leaving Vincent and I alone together.

"They will send no more? What will we do?"

"Do not worry, Little Cat. I will make my own money soon from my artwork. You will see. I have improved so much, I am confident that someone will buy my new drawings. Theo has said that they are just the type that all of the Parisian artists would admire."

"Is Theo going to stop sending us money?"

"No. He is a true brother and will not abandon us. Everything will be fine."

Just then, we heard a choking noise. We stopped talking and listened harder. It was the sound of intense sobbing coming from the studio. The sobs were followed by the frustrated wails of an infant. Vincent and I looked at one another and raced into the studio to see what was happening. We found Sien in her favorite chair holding Willem to her breast. I could see her bones showing through the skin of her chest, and her breast sagged lifelessly against her ribs. Her face was wet with tears as she looked at us. Willem's face was red from crying.

"It is gone. It is all gone!"

"What is gone, Sien?"

"The milk. I can make none. Neither breast will produce anything. I have nothing to feed my baby."

Sien cried frustrated tears, and Willem wailed hungrily. Vincent and I stared at her, not knowing what to do. She opened her hands to us helplessly.

"We could buy cow's milk," I offered knowing that we had just received a handful of coins.

"We cannot. The dairy men are a pious group, and it is Sunday. None will be selling today," said Vincent.

I had forgotten that it was Sunday. We had planned to go to church services, but the package had arrived and distracted us. Most businesses would be closed today. We looked around at each other, but we were all at a loss. Meanwhile, Willem's voice became louder and more agitated. His little red face began to turn purple from the wails of hunger.

"They would not even sell to a hungry baby?" Sien asked.

"They are not at their stalls in the market today. Most travel into the city from their country farms. We have no way to meet with them to ask."

"What do we do?"

"There is something we can try. I saw some of the mining families in Borinage do this. We can soak some bread in water until it is almost soup. Then, we will feed it to Willem."

"Will he eat that?" asked Sien.

"If he gets hungry enough he will."

"We only have black bread in the pantry."

Vincent pondered this, but shook his head.

"It is not ideal, but I do not know what else to do."

Suddenly, an idea struck me like a wild fire across my mind. I ran out of the room and retrieved the bit of cake I had saved from my room. When I had saved it, I had done so to keep the cake for when I truly needed it. The need was obviously now even if I had not anticipated needing it so soon. I brought the cake to the studio and presented it triumphantly to Vincent and Sien.

"Perfect!"

"That is wonderful, Little Cat! Willem will be able to eat yet. Now, go fetch a bowl of water so that we might start the process."

I brought him the water, and we watched as he placed the cake in the bowl, allowing the water to disintegrate it slowly. Vincent stirred the mixture here and there with his finger until it was soupy mess. It was time to give it to Willem. We put him on my lap so that he would not ignore us and try Sien's breast again. Vincent put his finger in the mixture and tried to offer it to the infant.

At first, the child refused the cake soaked finger we offered him. He jerked his head away and cried. I tried to hold his arms down, but he thrashed about reaching for Sien with a look of confusion. His chubby face turned even redder with exasperation. She stood behind Vincent sobbing at the spectacle.

Soon, his belly got the better of him and he allowed Vincent's cake soaked finger into his mouth. His mood changed suddenly when he tasted the sweetness of it, and we were able to spoon the entire mixture into his open mouth as though he were a baby bird. Willem fell asleep with a full belly, and we breathed a sigh of relief.

Chapter Thirty

July second marked Willem's first birthday. To my great surprise, Oma was invited to our apartment to share in a small birthday party we were having for the occasion. We had been keeping our distance from her as Vincent had instructed. The time spent away from her was not easy. I felt lonelier than ever, and Sien seemed more lost than usual without Oma's anchoring influence. I was very excited to have her come for a visit, and I hoped that this was the beginning of a time of forgiveness.

When Oma walked through our front door, her face fell and I knew why. The place had fallen into disrepair and was only as clean as I could keep it. Vincent had been working so much the he was no help at all with the house work. We were all thin, Sien more so than anyone else. She had not produced any milk in weeks. The agony of it had left her deeply depressed. She rarely left her bed at all, and her drinking increased. Vincent tried to ignore it, but we all saw the empty bottles. Moeder was not making much of an effort to hide them anymore.

Oma looked at me and saw the bones showing through my skin. My dresses from last year were loose about the waist and shoulders. They were a little short on the bottom only because I had grown a bit taller. I knew what I must have looked like to her. I smiled at her as she handed me a nice loaf of bread she had brought for us.

Sien came in with Willem on her boney hip. She smiled at her moeder's scowling face as though she did not see it, and Willem reached for his Oma with an infant's giggle.

"There is the birthday boy," sang Oma as she took Willem from Sien and bounced him on her own hip.

I began to cut the bread in slices for us paying extra attention to put aside a few of the soft bits for Willem. After running out of cake, we had discovered that the hard crust of the bread is harder to break down into mush. The baby almost choked on it once or twice, so I saved the soft parts for later without anyone noticing.

Vincent joined us soon after. We all ate bread and the adults drank coffee. We had no sugar to add, so the coffee was black. I knew that Oma preferred her coffee sweet, but she drank the bitter liquid and said nothing. I smiled at her and tried to ignore the tension. It was just so nice to have her here with us again.

Later, Willem began to cry and wriggle in Oma's lap.

"It sounds like he is hungry," she said, handing the boy to Sien.

A look of guilt crossed Sien's face. She gazed at Vincent. A terrible quiet stagnated about the room.

"Is there something happening here? Sien, why do you not take the child away and feed him? He is obviously hungry."

The air was thick with silence and tension. I felt like I could have spooned it out of the air and spread it on my piece of bread like soft cheese. What would we do? There was no way to hide this now. I decided to interject.

"I have his food ready," I said bringing the bowl of water and bread soup over to Sien. I had prepared it while everyone else was preoccupied with conversation and coffee.

"What is this? What are you feeding this boy?"

Sien looked down at the bowl and then back up to her moeder. She hung her head like a child caught in the act of stealing.

"I cannot make milk for him anymore," she said solemnly.

"You cannot make milk anymore? What is it that you are feeding him? What is this mixture?"

"It is bread soaked in water, Oma."

She looked amazed and angry at the same time.

"Bread soaked in water? And he eats this mush?"

"When he is hungry enough. It is perfectly healthy and temporary until Sien gets her milk back," said Vincent from the other end of the table.

"When he gets hungry enough?"

Oma was beginning to be outraged. I could see a fire behind her eyes that threatened to burn down the entire apartment. I braced myself against what was about to happen.

"And what is wrong with cow's milk?"

"We were buying him cow's milk," protested Sien.

"Why are you not buying it anymore?"

"We ran out of money," I offered but immediately regretted it.

After a long pause where the only sound was little Willem's hunger cries, Oma stood up and made for the front door in a hurry.

"Oma, please do not go. Where are you going?"

She turned around and looked at Vincent and Sien the way God must look when casting judgment upon the wicked.

"I will return. I am going to buy my grandson some milk."

She exited our apartment leaving us to all stare at one another. We shared a myriad of emotions. Guilt, frustration, agitation, and even curiosity. The feelings were shared with looks alone. Only Willem filled the empty air with his voice.

It was not long before she returned to our apartment with two bottles of cow's milk. One was for me and the other was for Willem. Oma ordered me to drink mine right there in front of her. She would not have me saving any to share later. She wanted to see my belly full for once. I did as I was told as she handed the other bottle to Sien to give to Willem.

I imagine that it was the best birthday present he could have gotten that day. He drank it down greedily, like a man dying of thirst in a desert.

Chapter Thirty One

I had worried that Willem's birthday had made the situation between Oma and Vincent worse. They were definitely not friends, and the birthday party had shown the very worst side of our family. To my amazement, Sien told me that I was to go to Oma's for a visit three days after the party. I asked if she would go too, but she said that she was tired and needed to rest. Sien promised that she would go next time. It was a happy surprise.

That day, I saw Vincent as he left the house to go painting. The weather was nice, and the summer sky made for wonderful light when he did his landscapes. He told me to have fun at my Oma's, and I grinned like a fool. Everything appeared to be better.

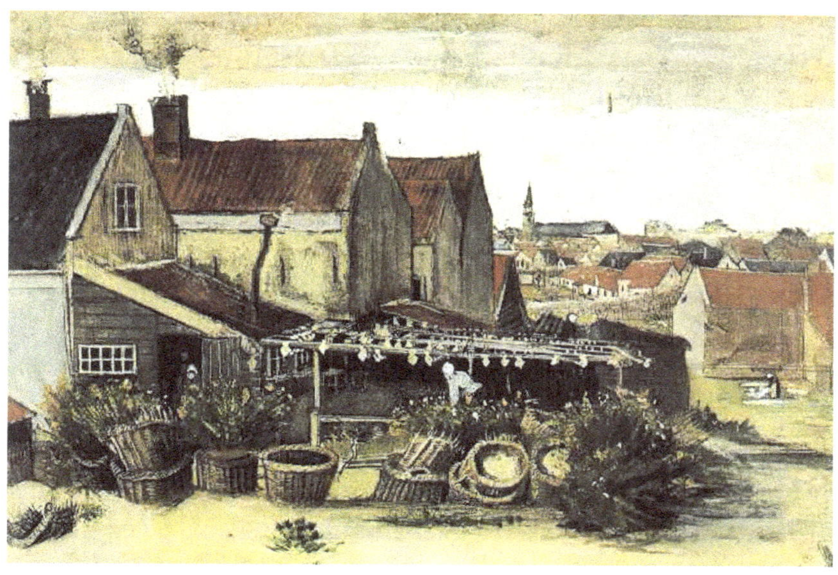

I started off down the street with a bounce in my step. The world seemed bright and happy to me at last. I took my time and enjoyed the stroll. It had been a while since I had had my Oma all to myself. Even little Willem had stayed home with Sien, so this would be a treat just for me. Perhaps she would have soft cheese for us.

I got closer to the fish drying house and the odor wafted across my nose. I had learned that by removing my bonnet and holding it over my nose, I could walk by the terrible place without vomiting. However, when I reached for my bonnet, all I found was my bare head. I had forgotten it at home.

I looked around embarrassed. Luckily, no one had seen me this way. I turned around and headed for home, covering my head with my hands anytime anyone passed me on the street. What an embarrassment this was to be in public, bareheaded as a vagrant.

I reached the apartment and ran inside. The whole place had an eerie stillness to it, the way homes do when everyone was asleep. I went into my room and retrieved a bonnet from the floor. It was not too dirty to be passable in public, so I wrapped it around my head quickly. The longer I was there, the more time I was wasting when I could be with my Oma.

Suddenly, I heard a noise in Sien's bedroom. I was not sure what it was at first, but it was a noise that was oddly familiar. The sound was familiar like an old nightmare was familiar long after you wake. I listened harder and heard it again. It was a grunting noise, like an animal. I walked over to her bedroom door and listened harder. The grunting came again and then a moan. With a sudden horror and disgust, I realized what was happening. Vincent was not here. I watched him leave.

My first thoughts were furious. The very idea that she could do this to us made my blood boil over. I saw red through the tears that filled my eyes. She was a terrible, vile thing. Shame filled me, and I wanted to scream.

I slammed my fists into the door.

"Whore!" I shouted with rage.

I heard scrambling on the other side, but I did not wait around for them to confront me. The last thing I wanted was to see the act as well. I ran to the studio, collected Willem, and raced out of the door bonnet in hand. There had not been time to tie it. I walked as fast as I could manage down the street towards Oma's house. I would not have Willem see our moeder that way. Whether he knew what he was seeing or not, I would not have it.

When we got to the fish drying house, I pushed his face to mine and put my bonnet over both of our mouths as I ran past the place as fast as I could manage with Willem on my hip. He squirmed a little under my arms, but I held him in place. We turned the corner to see Oma's front door shining like a beacon to us. I wrapped loudly on her door, and Oma greeted us with a concerned look.

"I was expecting you ages ago, Maria. Are you alright?"

I still had tears in my eyes when I hugged her with Willem in between us. He wiggled and fussed under the embrace, but I would not let him go.

Oma took the boy from me and sat him on the floor with a toy she kept at her house for him to play with. She put her warm arms around me and guided me to the kitchen to sit and drink a mug of water. Oma did not press me at first. I was allowed to sit there in silence for a minute and sip my water while I collected myself. After my sniffling had finally subsided, Oma put her hand on mine.

"What happened, Maria?"

My eyes began to tear again.

"Stop that. Whatever it is, you have wept enough for it already."

I choked back the tears and sat up straight in my chair.

"Moeder is prostituting again," I said in a grave tone. "I caught her. I was walking here, and I forgot my bonnet. I went back for it, and she was there with a man."

There were several breaths between us as we allowed the news to settle. It seemed more real now that it had been said aloud. The words tasted sour on my tongue.

"I know," said Oma.

Shock overtook me. I looked at her as though she were speaking some unknown language.

"You knew?"

"I set up the meeting. You were not supposed to see it, Maria. I never meant for you to know."

"You what?"

I was breathless. It felt as though someone had punched me in the stomach. Air was difficult to collect. The sheer madness of her words made no sense to me.

"Yes, I did, but you have to understand. I could not watch you starve any longer. Sien would not take a job with me at Pieter's house, so there was no alternative. No one else would hire her, not with her past."

"How did you…how did you arrange it?"

I was baffled. My Oma had somehow sent a man to our home to sleep with her daughter and pay her money. How had she even managed it?

"Pieter's mistress arranged it. She knows about such things, and she arranged the meeting through me. I arranged it with Sien."

Before I could respond, Sien burst into the kitchen red-faced and barely dressed. The sudden intrusion made Oma and me jump in our chairs. She looked at me with an angry face, and I wondered if her hair would catch on fire. Sien closed the space between us in a few strides and slapped me across the face. It happened so fast that the pain took a long time to hit me. When it did, my cheek burned and stung at the same time. I put my hand to it in shock.

"Sien!"

"I will not have my daughter calling me a whore!" she shouted in my face.

Defiance and rage burned through me, and I looked my moeder in the eyes.

"It is not a lie. You are a whore."

Sien pulled her arm back to strike me again, but Oma stopped her.

"Enough, Sien! Maria saw something traumatizing. Leave her alone."

We refused to break our angry stare with each other. I would not be the first to look away no matter how many more times she struck me.

"I am doing this for you, you ungrateful swine," she spat at me.

"You will not for long once I tell Vincent," I retorted.

Sien's face softened, and a silence filled the room. It was one of the first times I felt the power of holding information that was truly important to someone. It forced people to pay you a certain amount of respect, but it was also a burden that weighed heavily on your heart. The truth was I did not know what I would do with this new knowledge, but I saw the weapon that it could become.

"You cannot tell Vincent," Sien said slowly.

"Why?"

I had softened too, but I was unwilling to release my defiant tone just yet. I stared into her eyes just as furiously.

"Maria, you cannot tell him this. If you do, he will be angry."

"He will be angry at you and not me."

Sien sighed and looked away. I won.

"Vincent will be angry with me, but then he will leave us. He has told me as much himself. He said that if I ever went back to my old ways, he would leave *us*."

My breath caught in my throat. I had not thought this through. The last thing I wanted was for Vincent to leave us. Our family would disappear and we would have even less money than we did now. We could not go back to the way things were before, not with Willem with us now. I could not bear to think of Vincent no longer being with our family. I had grown so fond of having him in my life. The art and the books too would all vanish with him.

"You do not want him to go away, do you?"

I shook my head. Everything hard inside me softened.

"Maria, you must keep this secret with us," said Oma gently. "Your moeder has to do this so that your family can eat. We must keep it from Vincent for his own good."

I heard what they were telling me, but I struggled inside. I was an honest girl. Lies never sat well with me. And Vincent, he was my best friend. How could I tell such a lie and keep such a secret from a friend? What sort of person would that make me? The burden of this knowledge felt like a sack of potatoes on my chest crushing me with its weight.

"This will not be forever, Maria. When Vincent begins to make his own money, I will stop."

I said nothing and stared at the space between the women in front of me.

"Maria, do you understand us? Will you keep our secret?"

I took a deep breath and swallowed against the tension in my chest. What choice did I have? What other choice had they given me?

"Yes, I will keep this secret. I will not tell Vincent."

Chapter Thirty Two

It went on that way for a month. The weather was beautiful, and the light was brilliant, so Vincent continued to leave the apartment to paint. Whenever he would, I was to take Willem and walk to Oma's house. We stayed there for a few hours before I gathered up Willem and walked home with him. In the time I was gone, Sien would entertain visitors that were arranged by Pieter's mistress.

I tried not to think of it, but the task of denial proved far too difficult. The guilt of knowing about Sien's betrayal made it feel as though I were the one betraying Vincent day after day. We had more money for bread and cow's milk, but I had lost much of my appetite. The worry sat heavy in my stomach like a brick and made eating an unappealing task.

When I would try to eat, I did it quickly so as to not think while I did so. I plugged my nose to not smell it as I shoved the food in my mouth. However, I often was plagued with a diarrhea that cramped my insides and dehydrated me terribly. Vincent worried that I had become ill, but Moeder assured him that all young girls go through such changes as they get older. I would be of a woman's age soon. Stomach cramps were often a side effect of a woman's change beginning in the near future. It was a lie, but what did men know of women's pains?

Oma often tried to cheer me by telling me scandalous gossip that normally would have made me laugh. I tried to react for her, but it was no use. I felt tired and burdened with a great evil, so I did not make very good company. She never stopped trying to amuse me, no matter how many sad glares I gave her.

Vincent never seemed to notice the extra money that we now had. To his credit, the money was not very much. Sien kept it aside and only added it to the family allowance when no one was looking. Whenever Vincent did comment on the extra coin we seemed to have, she would smile and act coy.

"I was able to negotiate a better price with the baker. He started selling us our bread much cheaper than before."

Of course, she took enough of it out beforehand to buy more liquor for herself. Between using money Vincent did not know about and having the free time during the day, Sien managed to sneak liquor into her room much more efficiently than she had before. Only I knew the truth, and it was eating me alive from the inside. I envied Willem with his infant ignorance.

One day, Mr. Zuijderland came to the house to model and to continue our lessons. I was happy to see him, but the turmoil inside of me kept me from participating as I normally would have. I kept getting distracted by the swirling motion his coffee after he stirred it or the way the breeze from the open window moved the papers on the walls just so. Even though I was now reading and understanding whole pages by myself, he could tell I was distracted.

"Is everything alright, Maria?"

His kind face peered at me with genuine care and worry. The guilty brick inside my belly turned at the thought of lying to yet another friend.

"No, not really."

"Well then, tell me the trouble. Perhaps I can help."

I sighed and looked away at some papers that were rustling against the breeze.

"I am afraid that I cannot tell you."

"Oh? A secret, is it?"

"Yes," I said glumly. "It is a secret and not one I want to keep."

"Then why do you keep it?"

"Because I must, but it makes me feel terrible inside."

"Ah, I see."

He sat up and pulled me closer to him so that I was standing next to his knee.

"Those are just the worst. I take it that someone is putting you up to this secret keeping? Of course they are. Why else would you keep a secret you do not want to keep?"

"Yes. They are making me keep it, but I do not want to. I hate them for making me do this. I am sick over it, and they do not seem to care."

My brow furrowed with anger.

"I can see that, Maria. It hurts to be made to do things, especially when it's lying. Might I suggest a way to look at it?"

I nodded at him.

"Well, it is easy to judge people for their mistakes, but we all make mistakes. It is difficult to understand why people do certain things unless you have been in their exact position. Have you ever been in their exact position?"

I shook my head no.

"There, you see. Try to look at this with the idea that judging them is a pointless endeavor since you have never faced their exact situation yourself. Remember, people are strange. Of all the animals on earth, we are the strangest creatures I have ever encountered. You will find life a bit easier if you try not to judge when you can help it."

I pondered what he said for a moment before he started chuckling to himself.

"But, of course, here I am judging you for judging them. As you can see, I am an old fool who does not take his own advice. Must be all that old people air they make me breathe."

He poked my ribs with a smile, and I laughed. It was probably the first time I had laughed all month. I was so thankful to Mr. Zuijderland for it.

"What have we here?"

We turned around to see Vincent smiling at us from the doorway.

"It looks like we a couple of conspirators in my studio. Plotting intrigue are we?"

"Only minor intrigue, I assure you," said Mr. Zuijderland patting my head.

"The light is hitting you both so nicely today," said Vincent while he stared at us with his artist concentration. "Mr. Zuijderland, would you be opposed to staying a bit later and posing for me again? This time with Maria?"

"That is fine with me, sir. How would you like us to pose?"

"Just like you are. The way you are is perfect."

Vincent scrambled around the studio to set up his work station in front of us. He asked us to look serious, but Mr. Zuijderland kept smirking and making silly faces at me. This would cause me to giggle, and Vincent would chastise us for moving.

I felt lighter that afternoon modeling with Mr. Zuijderland in the light of the studio window. In between silly faces, I tried to think about what he said. I had never had to make a decision like Sien, so perhaps I should not judge her. It was a hard thing, though, not to judge someone who has hurt me. I promised myself that I would practice that very night until I got it right.

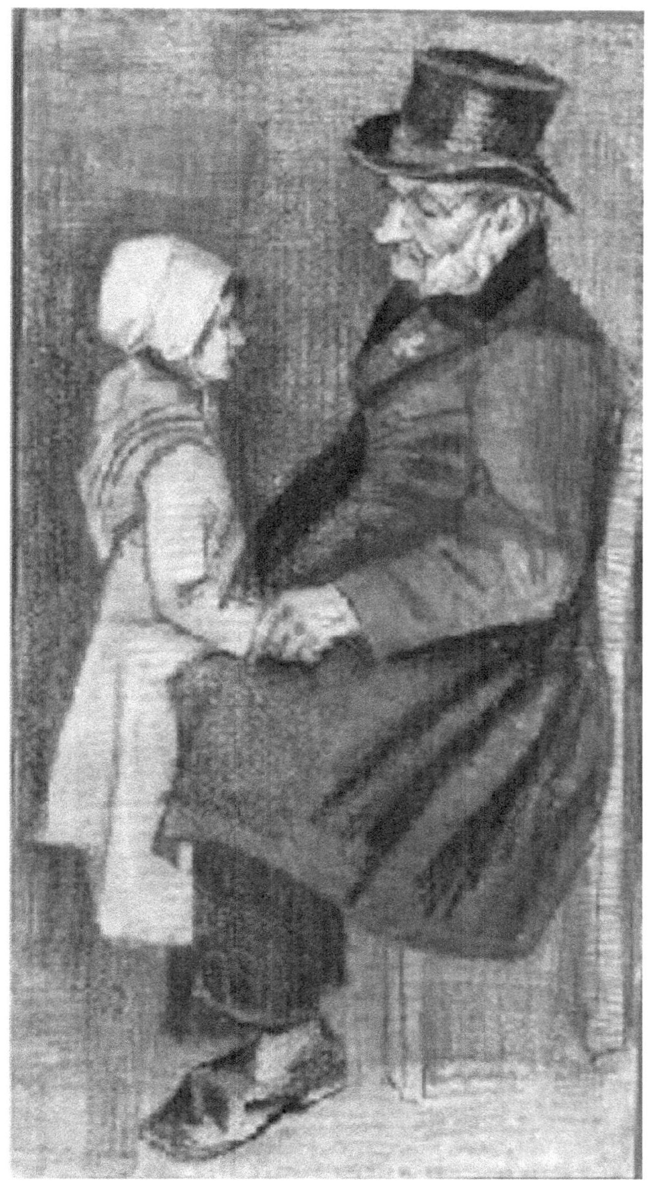

Chapter Thirty Three

It was a Saturday afternoon when a man came to our apartment.
I did not recognize him, but he addressed Vincent as though they
knew one another. Sien had taken Willem to the market, and I had
stayed home because I was feeling unwell. Therefore, as the only
lady of the house present, I entered the kitchen to make myself
known.

I did not address him nor did he look my way. I had thought
about greeting him as I would any guest, but something in his
demeanor told me not to. Something about him told me to stay
away. Instead, I contented myself to stand by the table quietly in the
event Vincent needed something from me.

"Good day, sir," said Vincent to the man.

"Yes, good day."

His voice was gruff and filled with possible malice. Something
was terribly wrong here. My muscles tensed all over.

"What brings you here? The lamp you repaired for me works
marvelously now. The light is a huge help. Thank you."

"I am here about the crockery."

"The crockery?"

"Yes, the crockery I sold you when you came to my store for
the lamp."

He was becoming more agitated. Finally, Vincent began to
notice the man's demeanor and stepped back from him a few steps.

"Yes, I remember that. It is a nice piece. My woman likes it
very much."

The man huffed and slammed his fist down on the table.

"You never *paid* me for it!" he screamed shattering what peace was left in the room. "I fixed your lamp, and you paid me. You took the crockery and never sent the payment you promised."

Vincent was in shock and stuttered a bit before he spoke.

"Sir, I am afraid you are mistaken. I sent the payment along with your boy. Carolus, I believe his name was. He came by the day after I left your store. I gave the lad the money to give to you."

The man eyed Vincent suspiciously.

"I have no boy named Carolus who works for me. I believe you are lying."

Vincent stood upright suddenly. His hands balled into fists at his side.

"I am no liar, sir."

"Well, I am calling you one."

"Then I will insist that you leave."

In a quick movement, Vincent grabbed the man's shirt and attempted to escort him physically out of the house. However, the man was far larger than Vincent and he turned the table on him with little effort. A fight ensued. Vincent tried to hit him, but the punch landed dully on his broad shoulder. The man grabbed Vincent by the throat and threw him against the wall, knocking over a small desk with some papers. He then pushed Vincent to the ground and began kicking him violently in the stomach.

I gaped in wide-eyed horror. Thoughts raced through my mind about what I could possibly do to help my friend, but there was no way I could overpower this man. Vincent wheezed and coughed up a little blood, and I knew I had to do something. I looked desperately around the kitchen for a crockery, any crockery that did not look old. I found a green and tan one near the stove that I had never seen before and raced back over to the struggling men. I sat the crockery on the table with a loud thud and looked at the man.

"Stop what you are doing!"

He stopped and looked at me.

"This is yours," I said as I pointed to the green and tan object on the table. "Take it and go."

The man stared at me as if he had just now noticed I was there. He slowly moved toward the table. I braced myself to run in case he took it in his head to beat me as well. He was big, but I was quick. I could outrun this man if I had a good head start. My whole body was tense, and I thought how glad I was that Sien and Willem were not here.

"Take this and go," I repeated more forcibly as I pointed to the door.

Much to my relief, he took the crockery and ran out of the door.

Vincent pushed himself upright and leaned against the wall. I hurried over to him, but he swiped me away. He did not look too badly injured, so I attempted to touch his ribs.

"Leave me alone!" he screamed at me.

I jumped back, feeling painfully hurt by his words. He started sobbing into his hands. I did not know what to do. Normally, I would sit with him or touch his shoulder if he was hurt, but he did not want me. I reached out again to try to touch his ribs. He was injured and needed help.

"Stay away! I have no want for anything. I have no want for painting. I have no want to live. What is my purpose in life for it cannot be this!"

Vincent continued to sob into his hands, so he did not see how his words made my face fall. I could not comprehend what I had done wrong. Should I have let the large man continue to beat at him? No answers came to me. Did I not do the right thing?

"It is bad enough that my father has abandoned me, and every art dealer in this city has refused me. Now, I am beaten by a dreg crockery pusher and saved by a little girl."

This was all that I could bear. I turned on my heel and left Vincent there to sulk in his own misery alone. It was obviously what he wanted. I would give him his solitude. If he wanted to wallow in self loathing, I would leave him to do so. However, before I shut my door, I uttered my defiant words to the empty air of the kitchen for it to judge however it saw fit.

"I am no little girl, Vincent. I am a Little Cat, and I do what I have to."

<h1 style="text-align:center">Chapter Thirty Four</h1>

The fighting between Sien and Vincent continued and worsened like a wound that would not heal. Vincent could sense that there was something wrong but did not have the proof of it. Each argument would end with tearful promises, like tiny sutures, made to one another to heal all. Just as tearfully, those promises were broken, and the horrid wound would be opened afresh spilling its poison into the world without regard. Its infection spread throughout the apartment, but I would not let it have me nor would I give little Willem over to it.

One evening, I awoke to an argument in the kitchen. Sien had thrown a glass that shattered against the wall, waking little Willem in his studio basinet. The baby wailed from terror, but no one attended to him.

I crept out of my room and hurried past the kitchen as to not be seen by Vincent and Sien. A Little Cat I was, silent as can be. The studio was dark, but I knew the room well, and the crying baby lead me directly to his basinet with his noises. I bundled Willem into my arms and ran back to my room with him.

He was not wet, but he was hungry and afraid. Sien still had not produced any milk, and we had given him the last of the soggy bread that evening. Willem tugged at my nightdress desperately seeking a breast from which to feed from. Of course, he found nothing but my thin chest. I turned him so that his head lain on my shoulder, and he cried harder. The fighting grew louder in the kitchen.

"Do you hear that, Madame? That is your child crying because he is hungry. A fit woman would be able to provide such a baby with milk."

"You do not dare lecture me about hunger. If you could provide us with food, my breasts would not be dry from my own hunger."

"Hunger? Did we not have bread tonight for supper? I noticed you somehow find the means to bring liquor into the house for yourself."

I put little Willem down on my bed and retrieved the wash basin I kept by my window. The bowl was cool and contained a small pool of water that shimmered in the moon light. I carried the bowl over to the bed with me and set it next to Willem's head. I laid my body down next to the screaming child and allowed my back to curl my body around him. We sank into the comfort of each other. Then, I dipped my finger in the water, and placed it in his mouth. He whimpered for only a moment before he began to suckle my finger as though it were a nipple. I held him tighter and we both felt relief in each others' embrace.

Willem was silent and whimpered only when I needed to add new water to my finger. Vincent and Sien never noticed. They only raged onward in the kitchen.

"How do you afford the alcohol, Sien? Where does the money come from?"

"I do not know what you mean."

"I know about it, Sien! How are you getting the money for it? Has your moeder been here? You know I have expressly forbidden her to visit us."

"She has not been here. If you ask me, you have no right to demand that she stays away. Maria loves her so."

"Maria knows that she can go visit her Oma, but that woman is poisonous to you. Your brother as well. They leak poison into your ears. No wonder you have turned out as you are."

"And now you will tell me how simple and stupid I am. I will not hear this again, Vincent. Not tonight!"

"How do you get the alcohol, Sien? Are you prostituting again?"

A silence in the kitchen stabbed at my heart. I held my breath in the darkness of my room and pulled Willem closer to me. I wondered if he knew.

"What does it matter? What does any of this matter?"

"Does that mean you are prostituting?"

"No, it means what is the point? I do not know why I bother to live this life any longer, Vincent. I think that I should just do the proper thing and drown myself."

"Sien, please do not talk this way. Not again."

"I am no good for this life, Vincent. Perhaps my salvation is not here on earth with you but in the river where God can forgive me. It is where I belong."

Vincent blew out a frustrated gust of air.

"I cannot have this conversation again, Sien. I think that you are just using this as a diversion. Are you or are you not prostituting yourself behind my back?"

"No, of course not. I promised you."

"You promised me a lot of things, Sien."

Vincent's voice had a lot of doubt but a lot of hope as well. I could tell he desperately wanted his fears to be untrue. He wanted Sien to promise him again to solidify his feeling. He knew nothing to be fact.

"This one is true. I am not prostituting myself. I have not done so since the day I met you, Vincent."

Her voice was soft and reassuring, even if it was a lie. I exhaled the breath I had been holding.

"Sien, you must change. You must promise me that you will change. You must put away the bottle and promise that your former life is behind you. I will move us to the country. Everything is more affordable in the country, and the air will cure us. It will cure our misery. You will see."

He sounded hopeful.

"Yes, Vincent, the country."

Moeder sounded beaten. I never saw Vincent strike her before, and I had not heard a struggle tonight, but her voice sounded as if she had been tied to a post and flogged repeatedly. She was a woman defeated in all respects.

"Promise me, Sien. Promise you will change, and we shall go to the country and be a family."

"I promise, Vincent."

I knew immediately that it was a lie.

Chapter Thirty Five

It was a Wednesday afternoon, and the air smelled like rot. Oma had always told me that when the air smells rotten, you knew that rotten deeds were afoot. It was a day that was usually better spent indoors. I did not have the luxury of staying indoors since it was a day that I had been sent to my Oma's house by Sien. She had not stopped prostituting from our home as she had promised Vincent, but at least I was not made to stay and pretend. Vincent had gone out to paint landscapes that morning.

I sat in Oma's parlor reading a small book that Mr. Zuijderland had lent me. It was about a count and a dungeon, but I could not really understand much of it. As I tried to read more, my thoughts were elsewhere.

Oma came into the parlor and handed me a pinch of bread. My stomach grumbled at the sight of it, but I chewed it slowly, savoring every bite. She had no cheese. I had already asked.

"What is on your mind, Maria? You seem to be oceans away."

I looked out of the window sadly.

"I do not know. I think it is because I hate what Moeder is doing."

"Maria, I know it is difficult, but we have discussed this. I know you love Vincent, but he cannot provide enough for you both."

"I know," I moaned. "I just wish that there was another way. She uses most of the money to buy alcohol. Did you know that?"

Oma sighed and looked down at the floor.

"I never said that my daughter was the sensible type. She always has let her feelings rule her. Sien gives into her impulses like a child, and she probably always will."

Thunder rolled across the horizon and made the window tremble as I gazed at the darkening afternoon sky. Rain was eminent. I could smell it through the rot. Large droplets slowly began falling from the sky and splattered against the window glass. I allowed myself to fantasize that whatever male visitor Sien was expecting was leaving his house at that moment only to turn around and think better of it when the rain soaked his hat. I smiled to myself at the thought of the man soaked and unable to meet with Moeder. It truly was a day best spent indoors.

Just then, another roll of thunder moved over The Hague. With the sound came the worst realization of my life. It burst into my mind like the lightning that spread across the clouds outside like God's feathering fingers.

"Oh, God," I said out loud.

"Maria, what is it?"

My heart quivered in my chest and promptly sank into my belly. The blood rushed away from my face, and I suddenly felt faint. The rain fell harder against the window adding further insult to my realization.

"Maria! Are you ill? Maria, answer me!"

I stared agape at my Oma, not knowing what to say. My mouth hung open like the fisherman's catch. I heard her but it sounded as though she were speaking underwater.

"Maria! You must answer me, girl. Do you hear me? I will have to slap you if you do not answer."

She was practically shouting in my face. I said the only words I could muster.

"Vincent went out to paint."

Oma stared at me perplexed. She shook her head to show that she did not understand. I had no time for explanations. I had to act now. He had gone out to paint.

I jumped to my feet, startling Oma to move away from me. Without another word, I ran past her, through the parlor, and out into the driving rain. My bonnet was soaked within minutes. The mud was building out of the dirt and water in the road. It threatened to steal the shoes from my feet, but I ran faster. My dress became heavier and heavier with wet as I trudged on. I was determined to reach the house before he did.

"Maria," shouted a voice behind me, but it seemed so far away that I paid no attention.

I held my breath as I rounded the corner at the fish drying house. Before I dared to breathe again, I ripped off my bonnet and pressed the wet cloth to my face. It sufficiently staved off the terrible odors enough for me scale the hill without vomiting. The mud was getting slicker by the second, so I stopped long enough to kick away my shoes into a nearby bush. I collected them in my arms and continued my journey.

My lungs ached with the strain. My legs burned. I ignored it. I could not stop. I had to make it there before he did. I had to warn Sien. She would not think about the rain. She would not think that he would come home early to protect his canvases from the weather.

Mud splattered my dress and face. It made loud slapping sounds with every step I took. Mud had even seeped in between my toes. It was like running on flippers. My progress was sluggish. I felt like even Willem could run faster than this, but my legs refused to take me any faster.

Finally, I reached our apartment completely out of breath. I managed to run to the door right as I heard the screams. Sien was screaming, and Willem followed her shortly after with his own screams. A gruff looking man wearing trousers and no shirt hurried past me. He gave me only the briefest of looks before he ran out into the rain. His face had been flushed, and sweat dotted forehead. I glared at his back as he ran from the house. I knew then I had failed.

Sien's screams turned into sobs in the other room. I did not know what to do. I was truly a sight to be seen, bareheaded and barefooted as I was. Mud caked my feet and legs, and it speckled my body and face like a disease. I found myself standing outside my own doorway unsure if I should go inside for fear of tracking mud in the house. Ridiculous are the thoughts one has when one knows nothing else to do. I wondered where Vincent was.

He burst forth from the door then, and I had to back up to make room for him. His face was flushed and angry. Sweat soaked through his shirt in patches under his arms and around his collar. I had never seen him as such. Fear trickled down my spine like a water drip when he found my gaze, and my only instinct was to run. I dropped my bonnet and shoes and ran back the way I had come.

"Maria, stop!"

The command came out like a bark. It did not sound like him, not my Vincent. Without thinking, I stopped. He was behind me in a second, and he grabbed my shoulders and spun me around violently. I wanted to cry out but did not. Fear kept me silent. Vincent knelt in the mud in front of me and stared into my eyes. His gaze hurt, and I wanted to cry.

"Did you know?" he asked as she shook me.

I cried out with a whimper.

"Did you know?"

Rain poured down on us from heaven soaking us through and through. Everything around us smelled of rot. Mold and rot and lies. My hair was now a mass of wet ringlets in my face. I did not know how to answer him with his face so full of rage as it was. This was not my Vincent.

"Maria!"

"Yes!"

He stopped shaking me and released my shoulders.

"Yes, I knew," I whimpered.

He stood up without breaking away from my eyes. The anger seemed to seep away from him only to be replaced by sorrow and betrayal. This was far worse than the anger. Tears welled up in my eyes, and I began to cry. I knew then that I should not have lied. I should have never lied to my friend.

"Why? Why did you not tell me?"

He began to back away from me with a disillusioned look about him. Terrified, I took a step toward him and reached my hand out as if to grab the air in front of him.

"It was because of her. Because she made me keep it from you. She said…she said that you would leave us if you knew."

My explanation came out as pleading, but he still backed away from me.

"Please, Vincent, I told her to stop. I begged her to stop. Please know that I just did not want you to leave us!"

All of the anger had drained from his face. Only sorrow lived there now. Sorrow…hurt…betrayal.

"Now, Little Cat, I will leave. There is nothing keeping me here any longer."

He turned his back on me and walked away. Vincent stormed off toward the horizon, away from me and away from our home. The rain poured down on him, and he slumped against it as he trudged across a nearby field. He never bothered to look back, not once.

I fell to my knees in the mud and cried until my eyes swelled. I choked in the rot and knew that today had ruined our family. I had hurt my friend, and now, he was gone forever.

Chapter Thirty Six

Vincent stayed in the apartment with us another week until travel arrangements could be made to send him to Drenthe. He had family there who could take him into their house until he found his own way. His uncle bought him the first train ticket to Drenthe that was available. Vincent had one week before his departure, so he stayed with us and slept on the sofa in his studio.

Sien kept her distance from him. She kept her distance from me as well. Neither of us wished to converse with her, and she conducted her daily business in the shadows like the shamed woman she was. Little Willem was her only company after I had gone through her room and smashed all of her hidden bottles against the wall. Sien had not even tried to stop me while I took my rage out on her supply of sin. I was determined to leave her with no liquor to soothe her conscience.

I tried several times to talk to Vincent, but he treated me like I was not there. I wondered if he thought my wrong doing was just as bad as Sien's. He had pontificated so often to me about purity of forgiveness, yet he was so reluctant to give any.

The afternoon before he was to leave for Drenthe, I crept into his studio to find him sulking among all of his possession packed in cases and stacked all around him. He was sitting on his sofa with his head in his hands. I was afraid to speak to him, but I was not sure when I would ever get another chance.

"Vincent?"

He looked up at me with tired eyes swollen with tears.

"Please do not leave. I am so very sorry for not telling you. You are my friend, and I should have told you."

He began to cry anew, and he gazed at me in the way he used to. It was a gaze of love and admiration, and my heart soared to see it. He opened his arms to me, and I ran into them. We never were much for affection, but it felt good to be held. He smelled like charcoal and sweet tobacco, the way I always remembered.

"It was not your fault, Little Cat. What were you to do? I am sorry that I blamed you so."

I exhaled. A knot of tension released in my heart. His forgiveness washed over me like a warm bath.

"So then, you will stay? You will stay with us, and we will find Moeder a job. We can go to the country like you said. People do not know her there. She can clean houses somewhere and do more sewing. We can be a family."

He pulled away and looked at me seriously.

"No, Little Cat. I must go. I am glad that you and I could forgive each other before I leave, but the injury Sien caused me is too great. I am sorry, but I have to go."

Fresh tears welled in my eyes.

"You cannot leave. We are a family, Vincent. Family does not leave. Please stay. Or, if you must go, take me with you."

"Little Cat."

"I would not be a burden. I could cook your meals for you and help you choose the best paintings to show. I would help you. Please do not leave me here with her alone."

I held his warms hands and pleaded with my eyes.

"And what of Willem?"

"Willem?"

"Yes Willem. You would never leave little Willem here alone, would you?"

I looked down knowing I would never leave Willem. He was so like my own child.

"He could come with us," I said, but I knew that was even more preposterous than taking me along.

"You are the only thing holding this family together, Little Cat. I must say that you are one of the strongest people I have ever known, far stronger than me. It is not in your nature to run away, but it is in my nature to do so. I am a coward compared to you. The road is a place for cowards, not brave little cats. You must stay and keep them alive."

He patted my head, and I swallowed a mouthful of bitterness.

"You know what I need?"

"What?"

"I need a new exercise before I leave. I have heard that the greatest schools in Paris have their students draw a young person as they might look when they are older. It is a difficult thing to try. Would you like to be my model?"

"I do not understand."

"I will draw you the way I think you will look when you are a young woman."

I looked at him skeptically for a moment.

"Please, Little Cat, it will be the last time you get to model for me. I would like to think of you as the young woman you will become. That will be a nice way to think of you after I leave."

I sighed and consented. He sat me on the floor and wrapped an oversized shawl around my shoulders. It was one of Sien's, a woman's shawl. Then, he positioned himself on the sofa looking down at me.

"This is a really great perspective. Look up at me, but do not turn your head."

I did so, and he began to sketch. His charcoal moved fast, and I struggled to stay still for him. As he drew, my sorrow for his departure turned into resentment, and my resentment turn into scorn. I looked at the man drawing my features in a fit of fever, and I could not help hating him a little for leaving me. I knew that the wrong Sien had done him was horrible, but how could he go? Surely he loved me, and I knew that he loved Willem. Coward or no, if he truly loved us, he would stay.

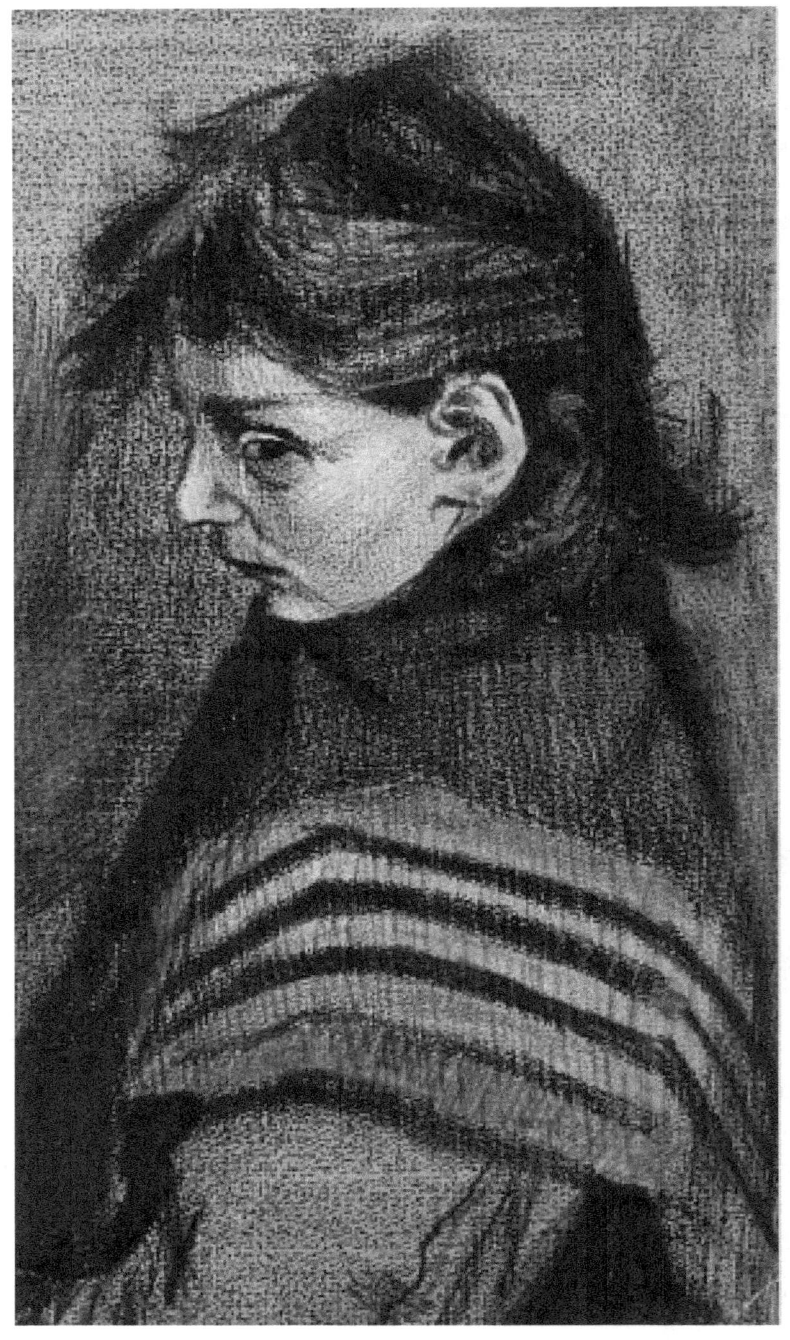

He finished quickly, and he coaxed me to rise and see his work.

"You always were a great model. Come look. This is how I see you when you are a young woman, Little Cat."

I looked at the drawing, and the first thing I saw was the scorn I had been repressing. One look into the face of this girl on the paper, and anyone would know that the person she was looking at had wronged her. She glared back at me with anger and reproach. It took my breath away. Did I really look that way?

"What do you think?"

Vincent knew what I was feeling, and he captured it on paper. No matter what I tried to hide, he saw me. He knew me. He was leaving me.

"I look…stern."

"You are often stern."

I pondered that statement and could find no real flaw in it.

"I look cross."

"I think you are cross. At least you are with me now."

I gazed up at him, and he smiled. I wanted to smile back but did not. It was so odd having the conflicting feelings of loving someone and being angry with them at the same time.

"You made my eyes too big, and I look old."

"Do you not like seeing yourself as a woman?"

"It is…disconcerting."

We both stared at the drawing together for a little while longer. Vincent put his hand on my shoulder. My voice softened as my anger ebbed.

"Thank you for not drawing me ugly like Moeder."

He leaned down and kissed the top of my head. I leaned into him as he hugged me closer. His smell wafted over me again in that comforting way.

"You could never be as ugly as your moeder, Little Cat."

Chapter Thirty Seven

I slept the sleep of the wicked that night. I tossed back and forth in my bed with nightmarish visions. Vincent would leave in the morning, and there was nothing I could do to stop him. That is what he said, at least, but perhaps he could be persuaded to stay. If I could devise a compelling argument to coax him to stay even one more night, I might possibly be able to keep him here with us forever.

All of my waking moments that night were spent plotting ways to make Vincent stay. However, none of the plans I thought about had any real chance of working. I thrashed around in my bed even more. I knew I had to think of something, but nothing solid came to mind.

As the morning arrived, so did a knock on the door. Vincent answered it and welcomed a man from the train station into the apartment. He showed him to the studio, and the man loaded Vincent's cases onto a carriage bound for the train station. My stomach felt a horrible dread. Vincent was leaving in a matter of hours, and there was no way to keep him from going. I rose and washed hastily in silence. I thought about talking to him privately again before we left, but he took his breakfast in his studio and kept the door locked.

Moeder rose and brought Willem into the kitchen. He cooed happily while I undressed and bathed him in a wash basin. He had no clue that our family was about to disintegrate. Sien did not speak to me. She did not even raise her eyes to mine. That was fine with me. I did not want to look at her anyway.

We dressed in out finest attire. I was fastening Willem's bonnet around his head when Vincent stepped out from the studio.

He was dressed in his travelling clothes, a white shirt, a grey jacket, and a grey set of trousers. My heart sank again, and I frowned.

We walked together to the train station while The Hague slowly awoke from its night's slumber. Roosters crowed from the roofs of hen houses. Cows bellowed their long laments to each other in the faint shadows of nearby trees. Children giggled as they ran to play in the morning dew of the grass wearing nothing but their night clothes. The air was crisp and clean and full of sound. However, we said not a word to each other, and the air around us sat heavy. Even Willem was silent as though he sensed that something was amiss.

The train station was far away enough to make my legs ache, but I did not dare to complain. Every extra moment I had was an extra moment to think of a plan. Thus far, the best idea I had was that Vincent would see all of us in our pitiful state and have a sudden change of heart. He would forgive Sien and promptly come back home with us. It was a far stretch to hope for, but it was all that I had.

We reached the train station and stopped at the platform. I began to tremble under the weight of anticipation. I was not sure what came next. To my left stood Sien, who held Willem in her arms. To her left stood Vincent. We stayed that way, in a wordless trance, for a few moments. No one looked at each other. It felt like an eternity.

When the train attendant called for the passengers to board, Vincent moved forward. I flinched noticeably. With a shock of horror, I thought for a minute that he would simply leave us there without as much as a farewell. However, he turned on his heel and addressed Sien.

"Sien, I wish to thank you for the happy times we had. I wish you could have left your past life behind so we might have started a new one together. That is not possible, so I must leave you now."

He sounded like he had rehearsed this speech for a few days. It had none of the emotion of his real voice and all of the superficiality of someone trying to mask something. Somehow, it sounded harsher than if he had used angry words. This way was just hollow. Sien had tried to stay composed, but she had begun sobbing into her handkerchief the minute he had finished his words.

"I wish you the best, and I hope you will find God's way."

Vincent was becoming visibly upset. I could tell that he, too, was finding it hard to keep his composure. When Willem cooed and reached for him, I saw several tears wet Vincent's cheeks and soak into his beard. He took the infant and hugged him before he handed him back to Sien.

"The apartment is paid for through the end of this month. You have until then to find something else," he said in a strained voice.

Sien nodded, unable to speak through her sobbing.

Vincent then moved toward me and kneeled on the platform so that we might be eye to eye with one another. I had so many emotions. I was hurt and filled with sorrow, but I was also angry. He was not going to have a change of heart. He was going to leave. Anger I knew how to show, so I drew my face away from him and refused to meet his gaze. This was all too much.

"Will you not look at me, Little Cat?"

I kept my gaze set firmly away from him.

"Please, Little Cat, I cannot go without a farewell from you."

"Then I will not look," I blurted. "If I do not look at you, you will not have your farewell, and if you do not get that, you cannot leave."

The sadness crept in and glazed over the anger. Hot tears welled up in my eyes, but I suppressed them from falling. Vincent reached out to me and took my chin. He turned my face toward his ever so slowly until our eyes met. He too was choked with tears and snot.

"Please," I whispered through the sadness. "Please do not go."

"I must go. There is no place for me here. I must go and find my way."

"There is a place. I will make a place for you."

He reached out, placed both hands on my shoulders, and looked into my eyes.

"Take care of them, Little Cat. Take care of them like I never could. Take care of them because you are the only one who can."

He squeezed my shoulders, and, in an instant, he was gone. Vincent rose and disappeared into the bowels of the train car with a movement so fluid, I barely noticed him do it. One moment he was in front of me, and the next he was not.

The tiniest of my hope for a change of heart had vanished. I stood there stunned that he had actually gone. A small part of me had sincerely thought that once it was time for him to go, he would not bear to be apart from us. He would turn around and come home. My hopes were dashed the second I saw the flash of grey that was his jacket vanish inside that metal belly.

Sien's sobs were drowned out by the whistle of the train as it slowly pulled away from the station platform. The black behemoth carried our Vincent away from us, promising never to return him. He was gone. He was truly gone.

Chapter Thirty Eight

After Vincent left us, I went to live with my Oma. Sien's sanity was more questionable than it had been before, and when she took her meager possessions and moved into a small room away from the family, Willem and I did not go with her. Oma knew that Sien would go back to prostitution. She would be a woman of the streets again. No other way existed for her, but Sien wanted better for us. She left me with Oma and Willem with her brother Pieter.

I was fairly happy with my arrangement because I had not forgiven her for driving Vincent away from us. I blamed her for so many things, even things that were not her fault. Sien became the symbol of all that had gone wrong for our family. I loathed her for it. She disgusted me, and I looked at her as such. Never again would I call her Moeder. As far as I was concerned, it was a title she did not deserve.

One drawback was that I never saw Mr. Zuijderland again. Oma thought it improper for an old man to spend time with a young girl, so he was never invited to our home. I sometimes looked across the streets when we went on errands hoping to catch a glimpse of him in public. Several times, I thought I had spotted him only to be disappointed by a man who merely resembled him.

Despite the loss of my teacher, I continued his lessons until I could read entire books by myself, including *Les Miserables*. I missed him, and the worst part of it was not knowing what became of the man. He had been seventy two when I met him. What other adventures might he still have with his time in the world? I thought about him often and liked to picture him by the sea reading a book and watching the boats sail past. I only hoped that he did not choke to death on the old people's air he was always running from.

When it came to Willem, I fought desperately against sending him to my uncle's home to live with the monster and his mistress. I could not have him growing up in the bosom of the devil. I railed against the decision to my Oma and insisted that he live in her home with us. She heard my pleas with patience and put her hand on my shoulder in comfort. This was a habit of hers when she was preparing to tell me what I did not want to hear.

"I understand your worry, but it is your moeder's wishes. Your uncle can give Willem a better life than I can. Sien knows I cannot afford to raise the both of you."

"Oma, we cannot let him go live with that monster."

"Take a breath, Maria. You will faint."

"I cannot see how Sien of all people would send Willem to Pieter!"

"I know what you are thinking, but remember, he is only a monster to girls. I have seen him with Willem, and he is fond of the boy. His evil is only for the girls, and you will live with me. Let Pieter's mistress take the brunt of the brute's evil. She seems to have a head for such things. My duty is to protect you from him, and he will raise Willem with a mind for business."

"We cannot possibly..."

"We can. We have no choice. We have no other life to offer the boy. Pieter will give the child a life. He will introduce Willem to a better life, and you and I will make sure he keeps his soul."

I tried to argue, but alas, I had no solution. If I had had the means to keep him, I would have. Even if I had hoarded every coin I ever found, I would not have been able to offer him anything else. I had no money and so Willem went to live with my uncle. I cried myself to sleep over the matter for months.

Pieter did seem to love Willem, and the boy grew without knowing the terrible pangs of hunger ever again. I wondered if his fondness came from the fact that, for one reason or another, Pieter never had children of his own. His divorced wife had proven barren, and his mistress never bore fruit either. We all agreed it was probably best in the event that he might have a daughter. I shuddered to think how he would have tortured such a girl. She would have had no one to protect her like I did.

Chapter Thirty Nine

Life continued the way that it does when a person is one of the survivors. Nothing more was to be said about it. As the years passed beneath our feet, we would hear rumors and whispers of Vincent. We heard scandalous tales of Paris and artistic bohemians, but not once did a letter come to us from Vincent's own hand. Perhaps he had forgotten the family he had for a short time. I never wanted to believe that. He was always present in my thoughts, so I assumed that I was always present in his.

In 1890, we heard the horrible news. On July twenty-seventh, Vincent Van Gogh walked into a field and shot himself in the chest with a revolver. He survived the shot and managed his way back to the Ravoux Inn where he had been staying. Vincent died two days later from the self-inflicted wound. He was thirty seven years old.

The story went that his beloved brother Theo hurried to be by his side and was there just in time to hear Vincent's last words.

"La tristesse durera toujours."

The sadness will last forever.

Theo died the following year. Theo loved his dear brother more than anyone else. He had supported him for most of his adult life. When Vincent died, a part of Theo went with him. He was said to perish from the sorrow of a broken heart.

I wept when I heard the news about Vincent. Oma patted my back and whispered soothing words to me. The pain of it was so tangible and infinite, I did not know how to cope. I had never lost anyone to death that I had loved so thoroughly. How did people survive this? I cried out what I could and buried the rest. I found a dark place in my heart and put the majority of my pain there to keep. I did not know what else to do with it.

Sien did not cry. I will never forget her face. We were sitting in Oma's parlor, and she heard the news as we all had, yet, she did not move. She did not cry. Sien stared into the air of the room as though she were dead. At first, I thought she was staring at us, and I beckoned her to come embrace us for comfort. She did not respond. She did not move. Sien stared at us and through us as though we were not there.

We called her name, and begged her to speak to us but received no answer. I checked her chest and found her to be breathing, and she blinked when I blew air in to her eyes. However, something left her at that moment, something she would never get back. I did not know this until later, but the news of Vincent's death stripped away the last bit of sanity she had left.

It was hard to continue to hate a person who had lost everything. I imagined that it was like hating a child who looked up at you with helpless need and unconditional love. Therefore, I released my hate for Sien as I watched her spiral farther and farther away from sanity.

When Willem turned twelve, Pieter begged Sien to marry one of her regular customers in order to give the boy a proper name. He wanted to begin Willem on a track to become an apprentice with some merchants he knew, but to hire a child with only his moeder's illegitimate name to call his own was outlandish.

The thought of marriage worried Sien to the point of fever, and Willem and I visited her in the hospital. She was delirious and speaking nonsense, so I asked Willem to leave the room so that I might speak with her alone. He was so sensitive, and I wanted to shield him from her insanity as much as I could. When he left the room, I leaned close to her.

"You should do this for Willem. I hate to agree with Pieter, but the boy needs a name. He would do better in the world with any other name than yours."

"You do not understand," she moaned.

"Will the man not have you?"

"No, it is not that. He wishes to marry me."

"Then what is it? Is he not kind? Is he ugly?"

"He is ugly, but so am I. He is old and kind and would be a fine enough husband for me."

"Then what is the issue? You would be fed, and you would no longer have to prostitute yourself for money. Why would you even hesitate?"

She sighed and looked away.

"I am already married to a dead man. I have the invisible ring of a widow."

I was silent for a moment as tears soaked her face. I leaned in closer to her and put my hand on hers.

"Moeder, you and Vincent were never married," I whispered as though she were a simple child.

At the time, I did not understand. I was honest, and what she had said was incorrect. I suppose that I thought she had taken leave of her senses again. As an honest woman looking back on this moment, I know that there are some things that are true in your heart even if they are not true in reality.

She waved me away and called for Willem. He came back into the room and I stood aside. Sien was ready to speak to him. This had nothing to do with me.

"Willem," she said with her eyes lolling back and forth. "I will do this for you, but you must always know who your real father was."

I cringed at what I knew she was about to do but did nothing to stop it. I was stunned into stillness. My mind told my mouth to protest, but nothing came out of my throat. Sien had lost the distinction between truth and want, and I knew what was coming next. I was too shocked to move or protest as Willem leaned in closer to hear her better.

"I named you Willem Vincent Hoornik because your father was Vincent Van Gogh. Never forget that. Never forget him. You are Vincent's son."

He nodded his head with tears in his eyes. I put my hands over my mouth to stifle a scream. I wondered what she had done and why she had done it. She had spoken the words he had wanted to hear. She had said what she wished was true. On many occasions throughout our lives, I tried to explain the truth to Willem, but he never did believe me. He thought that I was trying to undermine Moeder because of my harsh feelings toward her. The poor boy believed that lie until the day he died.

*   *   *

In 1901, Sien married Arnoldus Franciscus van Wijk as she promised, and Willem was given a respectable name. The arrangement enabled her to cease prostituting herself, but her spirits never lifted. She drank just as heavily, and her bout with insanity and depression worsened as the years rolled past her.

She spoke to us less and less. She muttered ramblings to herself that made no recognizable sense. Her husband ignored these oddities in his wife's behavior explaining them away as "her little quirks." He spoke of them like they were charming but moved her to Rotterdam and away from her concerned family all the same. We knew the truth. Sien had completely lost her mind.

In 1904, a messenger arrived to deliver the news to me that my moeder was dead. Sien had accomplished what she had always told Vincent she would do. She drowned herself. Clasina Hoornik had leaped in the Schelde River in Rotterdam and drowned herself. She was discovered washed ashore after the heavy stones she used to line her pockets had fallen out, allowing her body to drift downstream. She had been found by a local fisherman and his children. We buried her on a Sunday in The Hague where she belonged.

I wept for Sien as I had wept for Vincent, but only as much as I could. They were two people whose sorrow could not survive in this world alone. I felt powerless to do anything for them. What choice did I have other than to move forward and live my life? I put my sadness for her in that same dark compartment where I had stored the sadness for Vincent. All I could do for them was pray that they found peace together in heaven where there was no hunger and no sorrow. Perhaps they could marry there and live as they always should have, without judgment and without pain.

Chapter Forty

Despite all of my horrid uncle's thoughts, I never sold myself to men on the street for bread like Sien. Instead, I continued to read, and I learned how to write. That led me to learn how to count. Like words translated into sentences, numbers translated into bigger tasks like keeping ledgers and working bills.

When I was fourteen, I was offered a job with the butcher's family. I had applied to be a charwoman for their family home, but once they learned of my skills, I was quickly promoted to working their stall in the marketplace. The butcher himself was the only other person in the family who could read and track his daily ledger appropriately, and his eyes were growing old and unreliable.

The work days were long, and I was forever covered in the scent of thick, sticky blood. I often went home exhausted from the day, wreaking of sweat with hay and blood stuck to my dress. However, I did well at the job, haggling fair prices with the patrons who came to our stall. They began to know me as an honest woman, and my honest dealings were preferred over many others.

The butcher had two sons. The eldest had married a dairy farmer's daughter and they had a little daughter. His second son, named Gerritt, began courting me my first week at his father's stall. Gerritt was seventeen, and he had handsome features about his face even though his nose was far too large, like a small potato on his face.

It did not take long for me to love the butcher's family. They were all so kind and warm to me despite what they knew about my family. I worked without complaint for them in return. So grateful was I for their kindness that when Gerritt proposed marriage to me one autumn afternoon at my Oma's house, I did not hesitate to accept. Despite my early reluctance in regards to marriage, the comfort of his affections and his family's unwavering love enveloped me like a warm blanket. It was warm and safe and everything I always lacked as a child. We married with all of our loved ones around us on a beautiful day in September.

*   *   *

In 1906, I was thirty one years old. Gerritt and I had two handsome sons and a beautiful daughter that I named Clasina. I refused to allow anyone to call her Sien. The butcher had decided to spend his days at home now that his family was running the business. We worked long days along side one another and spent our evenings relaxing next to warm hearths. Our children played among the blood and hay at our feet and never wanted for their daily bread or meat to go with it. Everyone was fed and loved. Life was simple and happy.

I could not explain why I was always drawn to C.M.'s art gallery. I just was. A butcher's wife had no reason to stop and admire art, but I would take advantage of every chance I got to walk by the gallery and peer inside. It was as if an invisible thread connected me to the artwork, and I felt myself being pulled toward it like a horse on a tether. I often pondered the paintings I saw on display, judging them as I used to judge Vincent's work. I wondered if he would like the ones I liked or if he would have turned them down as not having enough Millet or Daumier for his liking.

Even though he was dead, I always thought of Vincent. It was like he lived with us and our family as an invited ghost in the living walls. No matter how happy and contented my life became, that old sweet sorrow for my friend never left me. He was a beautiful specter in his sorrow in a way I only learned to appreciate after he had died.

193

One afternoon, I had a house call to make. I never minded house calls even though they were normally for the infirmed or for the rich who lost their cook. This particular visit was to an almshouse where half of the elderly inhabitants were infirmed and could hardly walk. The proprietor answered the door and immediately began to apologize for his inability to pay his bill. I looked at the place, and I thought of Mr. Zuijderland. He had lived in a place much like this one. I sighed while thinking of my old tutor who was surely dead by now.

I stopped the man in his explanation and told him that he could pay me in eggs. I knew perfectly well that he had a rather large hen house next to his apartment, and he accepted the offer gratefully. We exchanged pleasantries before I left the almshouse with a straw basket full of eggs to take home to the family. My children loved eggs.

On my way back to the market, I decided to extend my journey by cutting across two streets so that I might pass C.M.'s gallery. I had not indulged my guilty pleasure for a fortnight and decided that I was due. It would be a treat.

The day had turned misty by the time I arrived at the gallery, and a heavy wetness hung awkwardly in the afternoon air. Something was strange. The air felt different. The sounds of the street traffic felt muffled. When a light dizziness settled in, I wondered if I was coming down with an illness. I shook myself and peered into the gallery window, hoping the artwork would break the sudden spell that had been cast upon me.

What I saw stopped my breath.

Colors. Colors were everywhere, swirling around each other like a storm. Such colors I had never seen. They were not the earth colors of life but the kind that you saw when you closed your eyes and dreamed. I saw scenes of Paris cafes and sunflowers. Next to those were peasants napping beside bales of hay, but the hay was painted like it was moving on the canvas in some unseen breeze. I saw a painting of a sky full of stars that swirled around each other. The visions whirled around me, and I feared that I might faint right there on the street. Everything was so alive. It was all so overwhelming. The paint *moved* on the canvases.

I was pulled from my trance when I heard a woman inside mutter a very familiar name.

"Theo."

I do not recall summoning my legs to move, yet they did. My arms were never told to open the door of the gallery, yet they did. Without my asking it to, my body carried me into the gallery as silent as the grave. I stood there watching a woman in black speak to the crooked figure of an aged C.M. Neither of them noticed my intrusion. The Little Cat I was again after years and years.

"You must buy some of these, dear Uncle. I am in desperate need of money. I have sold almost everything else. Theo would have never wanted me to sell his paintings by Vincent, but I have nothing else to do."

"Johanna, I do not think I have the space. No collectors want such odd paintings. We know the poor man had lost his mind. Just look at these."

They took a moment to review the paintings nearest to them before C.M. shook his head.

"I want to help you, but have you thought about remarrying? Your husband has been dead for many years now. It would help your money troubles."

"I am a widow, and I will stay a widow, sir."

As they argued further, I stared past them at the paintings that filled the parlor. So many colors. Such wonderful paintings. Could it be possible that my friend Vincent made these?

Then, I saw it. Directly in between the two arguing people in front of me were those steely eyes I knew so well. He was thin with high cheek bones and a reddish beard that was darker than his light hair. His serious brow was furrowed in a way only the truly serious people can accomplish. He had painted his eyebrows with blue and grey paint to add severity to his gaze. His shirt and jacket had barely been painted in as though they were an afterthought, and it blended into a speckled background of blue, red, and black. Everything forced you to look at his eyes which were solemn and serious. He gazed out from the canvas trying to convey his life, his loss, and his sorrow.

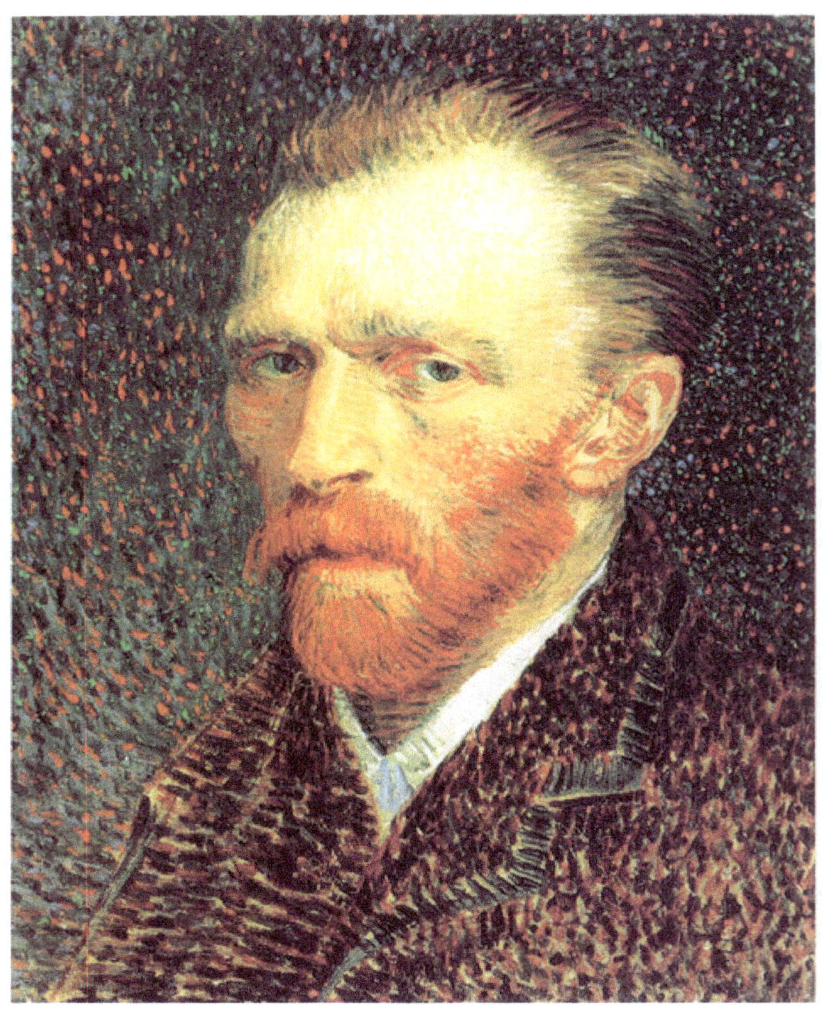

It was him. It was Vincent. It was my friend.

Sadness welled up inside of me. My heart began thudding heavily against my chest. I tried to breathe, but I forgot how. My face grew hot, and in my panic, I dropped the basket of eggs I had been carrying on the floor. The sickening sound of cracked eggs filled the room.

"Oh!" yelped Theo's widow.

They both spun towards me with perplexed looks on their faces. My basket had made my presence known to them, and now they stared at a woman unable to catch her breath. I put my hand to my chest because it felt as though it was going to burst. The broken egg yokes seeped through the basket and began to leak onto the floor. I had no room in my brain to be embarrassed.

"Madame, can we help you?" asked C.M. as he moved toward me ever so slowly. He looked like he was trying to approach a frightened animal cornered in a room.

I shook my head violently at them and drew in a ragged breath.

"I am sorry," was all that I was able to say before I grabbed the basket from the floor and ran out of the gallery.

It was raining now, not hard enough to soak but enough to mist. I hurried across the street and ducked into an alleyway where I knew there to be cover from the rain. The ground had already been muddied, but I sat in it anyway and leaned my back against the wall behind me. My chest heaved up and down with the exertion of regaining my breath. I tore off my bonnet to allow for more freedom.

As soon as the pain left my chest, and I was able to breathe once more without gasping, I began crying. The tears were hot and soaked my face quickly. Every ounce of repressed sorrow leaked out of me as though there was a hole in my body. My very soul spilled out onto the alley floor. I wept like the child I had never let myself be. I wept like I should have wept when he left us that day at the train station. It was the untamed crying of a woman truly unable to contain herself any longer. I wept like I should have when Vincent died. I screamed into my hands and balled my fists with rage. Mud seeped into my skirts from beneath me, and I kicked at it as though I was being attacked. I tore at my clothes and hair and wept like I should have when Sien died.

I unlocked the dark part of my soul where the sadness for Vincent and Sien slept and let it pour out of me into the mud all around me. It was the sort of grief that only insane people understand. This was the kind that tears away all hope you ever had that you would ever recover. It was grief that ends a part of your soul and reveals a child inside that you thought had died at birth. When I closed my eyes, I saw only the painting of his face, and I wept even more.

"Vincent," I choked out through my ragged sobs. "You finally painted something beautiful."

9 781938 230622